SECRET

AUSTIN

A Guide to the Weird, Wonderful, and Obscure

Les Thomas & Cheryl Thomas

Library of Congress Control Number: 2020938247

ISBN: 9781681062815

Design by Jill Halpin

All photos provided by the author unless otherwise noted.
Cover: Bevo, Cal Sport Media/Alamy Stock Photo

Printed in the United States of America
20 21 22 23 24 5 4 3 2 1

For Charlotte, Jack, and Sawyer, who were born to love Austin.

CONTENTS

VI

INTRODUCTION

William Sydney Porter, a short story writer known as O. Henry, called it the "City of the Violet Crown." It looks that way on a bright spring day when bluebonnets line the roadways into town and the sun rises over the rolling hills. A river runs through it...so does poetry and music. Some of the darndest things have happened here. A soldier left for dead on a Civil War battlefield came to Austin and helped build a world-class university. A hopeless writer, who'd just lost his wife, was found guilty of bank embezzlement. Now the courthouse is named after him. Everyone thought a wildcatter's well was a lost cause. It came in a gusher—funding higher education for generations. When other growth stalled, a student moved into a college dorm room and invented the Dell computer company. Turned off by Nashville, an outlaw named Willie sang his way far past the Austin City Limits. All roads led to SXSW, named for an Alfred Hitchcock thriller, *North by Northwest*. Even bats, unloved in other places, found thousands of new friends in Austin.

Secrets whisper all around you. You can find the world's first photograph and the oldest flying dinosaur. Beneath the nation's only Moon Tower lights, Janis Joplin sang her first songs and Hank Williams sang his last. Actress and model Farrah Fawcett invented big hair and dreamed even bigger dreams—of becoming an artist. A century after prohibition ended, a geologist built a moonshine still and became one of the nation's biggest vodka producers. Whole Foods reinvented the grocery store.

If it hadn't been for Austin, bluebonnets might not even be the state flower. It could have been prickly pear cactus, except for the intervention of some determined Austin women. It's a city where it's OK to be a slacker or a cutting-edge entrepreneur. Stop for a burger at the drive-in where actor Matthew McConaughey said it first on screen, "Alright, Alright, Alright."

ALRIGHT, ALRIGHT, ALRIGHT

What do you say when a drive-in makes you a movie star?

One of the most famous lines in movies was first spoken when an unknown actor who had never filmed a movie scene before wheeled into Top Notch Hamburgers, a hangout in North Austin. He parked next to a car full of girls and spoke a line he had just made up. That would help make him famous: "Alright, alright, alright." Matthew McConaughey went on to a huge movie career, but Top Notch has hardly changed from its close-ups in 1993 when it was a backdrop for many scenes for Austin filmmaker Richard Linklater's breakthrough film, *Dazed and Confused*.

McConaughey was playing the part of Wooderson, a 20-something hanger-on who couldn't quite get over his high school days. He explained in an television interview on *George Stroumboulopoulos Tonight* that he was waiting for his first scene and listening to a recording of the Doors Live on the radio of the Chevelle he drove in the movie. "Between songs, (Jim) Morrison goes 'alright, alright, alright, alright'—four times," McConaughey recalled. "I thought, 'What would Wooderson be thinking about?' Four things—his car, getting high, rock and roll, and picking up chicks. I pulled up and—'alright, alright, alright.' Three out of four."

The dining room inside Top Notch features mementos from the movie, including a replica of the wooden paddle that Ben Affleck broke in a rage after a freshman prankster dumped a

Top: Top Notch Hamburgers looks much as it did when Dazed and Confused was filmed there in 1993.

Inset: The dining room displays movie props.

bucket of paint on him from a rooftop. It was also one of Affleck's first movie roles. Outside, the drive-in's oversized neon sign hasn't changed from the days when it lit up the big screen. The sleeper hit also gave movie audiences one of their first looks at Austin. But when customers roll into a parking space now, and speak into the intercom, usually it's just to order a burger.

The house featured in *The Texas Chainsaw Massacre*, a cult classic filmed around Austin, is now located on the grounds of The Antlers Inn in Kingsland after being moved from Round Rock.

TOO BIG TO DELIVER

Where can you make your own postcard?

"I like to make art that, when you die, your kids will fight over it," says Todd Sanders, owner of Roadhouse Relics, a neon art studio.

Sanders creates neon artwork that has been featured in movies such as Terrence Malick's *Tree of Life*. His neons also grace famous places, such as Continental Club in Austin and the Museum of Neon Art in Glendale, California.

One of the artist's most popular renderings, however, has been a humble postcard. As most Texans know, bigger is better. This giant painting does not disappoint. This vibrant paean to Austin was created on the side of Sanders's neon art and relic business in 1998 by the artist and his friend Rory Skagen. It is a throwback to pictorial postal calling cards from the mid-20th century. A ribbon with "Greetings From" lies on the "A," giving us a play on the ubiquitous Texas greeting "Howdy!" The huge letters of the name *Austin* are outlined in black and red to create a frame for important local landmarks: Congress Avenue Bridge, Barton Springs, the University of Texas Tower, and the state's Lone Star Flag. The large undulating letters hover over the capitol building. The point of re-creating a postcard love note to his city, according to Sanders, was to liven up an area that had seen better times. As outdoor art will do, the painting faded in the unyielding Texas heat.

Step up to the curb with your very best smile and put yourself in one of the most photographed backdrops in Austin.

The giant Austin postcard outside the Roadhouse Relics neon art studio is one of the city's most popular photo ops.

RETURN TO SENDER

WHAT The Austin postcard

WHERE 1720 S. First St.

COST Free

PRO TIP Bring some friends and a selfie stick.

In 2013, after a fundraising campaign, a renovation of the original was accomplished, providing travelers with a perfect backdrop for photos. After taking your photos, visit Roadhouse Relics for a lesson in how to create art using metal with bent glass.

THE BIG BYTE

How can overhead make or break a fledgling business?

Michael Dell took a different path to business success. Like Bill Gates, he entered college with a plan to graduate and begin a career. He had already been successful in such endeavors as selling newspaper subscriptions, earning five figures in his first year. However, 1983, his first year as a premed major at the University of Texas, took him down a pretty daring path.

It was the early days of the computer age, and Dell capitalized by building computer upgrade kits in his dorm room, No. 2713 in the Dobie Center. Filling his dorm room with cheap outmoded computers, he upgraded them with kits, selling them from the trunk of his car.

Dell's homegrown business flourished. Going ahead full steam against behemoth competitors such as IBM, he used the advantage of low overhead for his new business to bid on a state contract for computer upgrade kits. The entrepreneur in Room 2713 was charting a course for changing the world of computing. That

Michael Dell began to invent his computer empire in Room 2713 at the Dobie Center. The dorm has been home to other famous UT alumni, including actor Matthew McConaughey and former Florida governor Jeb Bush.

One of the earliest high rises at the University of Texas, the Dobie Center has housed a number of students who went on to fame and fortune.

was Dell's last year in a dorm room. He convinced his parents of the efficacy of his business with a one-page business prospectus, showing a 15 percent profit in year one. And just like Bill Gates, his college days ended early.

ARACHNOPHOBES, BEWARE

What do you do if you find yourself in the grasp of one of the world's biggest spiders?

Just keep walking. You'll pass right under *Arachnophilia*. Standing 23 feet tall and 35 feet wide, the giant spider towers over the Greenway Park hike and bike trail that encircles the Mueller retail and residential development, northeast of downtown. The trail, made of crushed granite rocks, is surrounded by artful xeriscape. Pedestrians will discover soft leaf yucca blooming fragrantly in the spring and summer, as well as native agave and grasses. These plantings are a feast for the eye as well as the nose.

As for Arachnophilia's purpose in this xeriscape, she's big, but she isn't meant to be scary. The giant spider stands in stark contrast to the common perception that all arachnids are fearsome creatures. Sculptor Dixie Friend Gay, who created the spider as part of the Art in Public Project in 2008, said her goal with each piece of art is to create a sense of "childlike wonder and exploration for neighbors of all ages."

A giant spider will let you "play through" on the Mueller Greenway Park trail.

One of city's biggest sculptures aims to make new friends for spiders.

The metal she chose will transform under the hot Hill Country sun and rust in the rain, turning a dark shade of orange. The arachnid has six deep purple unwavering eyes and guards her attached egg cocoon festooned in shades of blue and turquoise. Her presence underlines the city's desire to respect and preserve the ecology of the community. She's a giant friend of her community.

BEVO SETTLES AN OLD SCORE

Did the nation's most famous longhorn really get his name from a losing score?

The good news is that the Aggies didn't name Bevo, the beloved University of Texas mascot. The bad news is that they ate him.

Seared into Longhorn lore is the legend that Texas Aggies kidnapped the steer and branded 13-0, the score of a 1915 football victory, on his side. When the steer was returned to UT's Forty Acres, stalwarts altered the brand and coined the name "Bevo." It turns out that this may be a fumble of what really happened.

According to research by the Texas Exes alumni organization, the name was first used in the December 1916 issue of the Texas Exes *Alcalde* Magazine. Editor Ben Dyer gave an account of the introduction of the steer at a halftime ceremony and wrote, "His name is Bevo. Long may he reign!"

As it turned out, not very long. The first Bevo had an ornery disposition. He often charged photographers who tried to take his picture. The steer was fattened up and barbecued for the 1920 football banquet. To mend fences, the Aggies were invited, too,

---

Even if the origin of his name is unknown, Bevo turned out to have a much better ring than the name of the little tan and white dog that preceded him as a mascot. His name was Pig Bellmont, after Athletic Director L. Theo Bellmont and Gus "Pig" Ditmar, an offensive lineman who could slip through defensive lines "like a greased pig."

Bevo is one of the nation's most famous college mascots, but the origin of his name is clouded in mystery. (Cal Sport Media/Alamy Stock Photo)

and were presented with the side of the hide they had branded.

There's still a mystery about where Dyer got the name Bevo. One of the most likely theories was that it was a nationwide fad at the time to add an "O" to friends' names. So there was Harpo, Chico, and Groucho. And perhaps even "Beeve O."

BRAND NAME LONGHORN

WHAT A longhorn steer named Bevo, the beloved mascot of the University of Texas.

WHERE Bevo can be seen offering his solid support at football games.

COST Price of a football ticket

PRO TIP Bevo's massive horn spread has thousands of imitators with "Hook 'em Horns," UT's famed hand signal made with raised index and little fingers.

A GARDEN OLDER THAN DIRT

Where can you walk in a garden where dinosaurs once roamed?

Some gardens have scarecrows. Others, like Zilker Botanical Garden, have a dinosaur towering over the foliage, replicating what Austin might have looked like about 100 million years ago.

A life-size sculpture of an Ornithomimus (Greek for "bird-mimic") dinosaur greets visitors to the Hartman Prehistoric Garden. It's a replica of one of the dinosaurs from the Cretaceous period whose footprints were discovered in the garden in 1992. Paleontologists found more than 100 tracks made by prehistoric creatures in a part of the garden that was once a limestone quarry.

Built around those original tracks, which were recovered with dirt to preserve them, the Hartman Prehistoric Garden re-creates an ancient garden like the one dinosaurs once roamed. There are spore-producing plants, such as ferns, horsetails, liverworts, and gymnosperms (cycads, conifers, and ginkgos), and the first angiosperms (magnolias and palms). Many flowering plants are also thought to have evolved during the Cretaceous period, lasting from 145 to 66 million years ago, along with dragonflies, butterflies, and a wide variety of other insects. A moat around the garden's Dino Island is stocked with gar, an ancient type of fish that still exists. A shady path winds beneath towering cypress trees and palm trees that grow near a large refreshing waterfall.

Dinosaur tracks discovered in Zilker Park planted the seeds of a prehistoric garden.

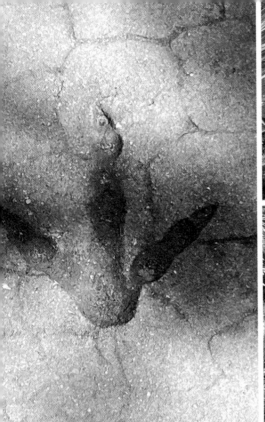

A life-sized sculpture of an Ornithomimus looms large over Dino Island.

It's an ancient garden, but it's designed to intrigue the youngest of visitors. There are animal-shaped boulders that replicate petroforms, rocks that Native Americans formed in the shape of animals, and a "forest" of petrified rocks that children can climb on.

GARDEN GUIDE

WHAT Hartman Prehistoric Garden

WHERE 2220 Barton Springs Rd.

COST Adults (Austin residents), $6, nonresidents, $8; ages 3-17, (Austin residents) $3, nonresidents, $4.

PRO TIP Signage is a little tricky at the garden. Get a map from the office to help you find your way to the Prehistoric Garden that's sheltered behind the Rose Garden.

DISCOVERING A PEARL

Where could you gas up and hear Janis Joplin sing?

They were unlikely friends. He was a yodeler who loved country music. She sang a whole new kind of music. A little jazz. A little blues. Mostly loud. And lonesome. Out on the Dallas highway, Kenneth Threadgill operated a service station unlike any other in Austin. Other stations had grease racks. Kenneth had a music stage.

Most Wednesdays, you could find Janis there, singing her heart out for $2 and free beer. The crowd loved it. Janis went on to play concerts where thousands screamed her name. She never forgot Kenneth. When asked to sing at his 60th birthday party in 1970, she cancelled a $15,000 concert in Hawaii and came running back to Austin. Kenneth was thrilled. Janis found a little piece of happiness, too.

Kenneth and Janis both passed on, but Threadgill's kept the music going. Austin music icon Eddie Wilson, one of the founders of Armadillo World Headquarters, restored the landmark and operated it as a restaurant and music hall for

JANIS JOPLIN AT THREADGILL'S

WHAT Threadgill's

WHERE 6416 N. Lamar Blvd.

COST Free. The future use of the site was still undetermined by mid-2020.

PRO TIP Kenneth Threadgill can be seen in a cameo role, singing with Willie Nelson in the 1980s movie, *Honeysuckle Rose*.

When Kenneth Threadgill opened the music stage after Prohibition in 1933, he stood in line all night to get the first beer license in Travis County.

An unknown Janis Joplin often performed at Threadgill's when she was a student at the University of Texas.

almost 40 years. He filled it with photos of Kenneth, Janis and Austin music memorabilia. All of it was auctioned to the highest bidders after Threadgill's was forced to close in early 2020 because of revenue lost to the COVID-19 virus.

A TEXAS-SIZE BAT

Where can you see the world's biggest bat?

Austin does not now subscribe to the belief that bats are terrifying or should be evicted. However, their arrival in 1984 brought with them a growing hysteria about bat attacks. The Congress Avenue bridge adjacent to the Austin American-Statesman complex had been renovated in 1980. Little did the city know that the nooks and crannies underneath the bridge would draw bats in record numbers for the purpose of nesting.

Just in time, ecologist Dr. Merlin Tuttle swooped into town, bringing with him his Bat Conservation International association and easing citizens' fears with a concerted "love your bat neighbors" campaign. Now Austinites brag about their faithful colony of 1.5 million Mexican free-tailed bats. It's reputed to be the largest such urban colony on earth. Enjoying the city's moderate climate and ample supply of insect food along rivers and lakes, the bats generally arrive in March and escape the Texas winter for friendlier climes farther south in October.

To honor this mammoth population, the Downtown Austin Alliance bankrolled a Texas-size bat sculpture made of dark aluminum. The art piece, which is a part of Art in Public Places, was created by Dale Whistler. Situated on South Congress

---

NIGHTWING BAT SCULPTURE

WHAT A Texas-size tribute to Austin's bat population

WHERE 300 S. Congress Ave.

COST Free

PRO TIP *Nightwing* represents the city's love of bats as seen in the bat mascot for the city's former ice hockey team and Bat Conservation International, an active Austin nonprofit organization.

A giant bat sculpture perches near the Congress Avenue Bridge, where more than one million Mexican free-tailed bats hang out.

Avenue in the middle of a traffic island, the bat with its massive wings measures 18 feet tall and 20 feet wide. It turns with the breeze to give everyone a view of the bat. The Austin bats do the same acrobatic maneuvers every warm evening.

The sculpture rotates 360 degrees to give viewers a chance to see its beauty in flight.

CUSTER RODE TO THE RESCUE

Dashing and daring, George Armstrong Custer was a nemesis to the South during the Civil War. How did he become a hero to Texans?

Many still call it the Custer House. The handsomely restored, two-story brick-and-limestone house is officially the Arno Nowotny House, and today it's the headquarters for the director of the Dolph Briscoe Center for American History. But George Custer and his wife Libbie called it home when the famous "boy general" of the Civil War was assigned to keep order in Texas just after the end of the war. Custer endeared himself to Texans when he ordered his troops not to forage goods from locals or to destroy their property. Several soldiers who violated the order were whipped and shorn of their hair.

He and Libbie loved Austin. They took leisurely horseback rides around the countryside. Libbie enjoyed the simple comforts of the spacious Italianate-style house that formerly served as the Texas Asylum for the Blind. Among other niceties, she was glad to have a bathtub.

In 1865, Custer posed with his officers and their wives for an informal portrait on the main porch. The house was restored in 1984 when its extensive south-facing porches were rebuilt. The house is listed on the National Register of Historic Places. Built by Abner Cook, who also built the governor's mansion, it's part of what once was known as the Little Campus. It is now called

Built in 1856, the house where Custer and his wife Libbie lived after the Civil War is one of the oldest buildings on the University of Texas campus.

Left: Custer was a popular figure during the time he spent in Austin. Photo from Library of Congress, Public Domain Archive (www.picryl.com).

Right: Custer and his wife Libbie lived in this house after the Civil War.

the Herman Sweatt Campus, in honor of the pioneering Houston civil rights activist whose landmark lawsuit helped him become the first African American admitted to the University of Texas Law School just after World War II.

Ten years after he left Austin, Custer rode off to his fateful death at the Battle of the Little Big Horn. His friends in Texas were stunned and saddened. "Texas deserves the honor of attempting to wipe out the Sioux," the *Austin State Gazette* declared. The legislature passed a resolution of condolence saying that Custer had "endeared" himself to Texas by his service.

BOOKS WITH A VIEW

Where can you find the city's most relaxing reading space?

The rooftop garden at Austin's new Central Library wins hands down. Stately live oaks and other native trees shade lounge chairs and comfortable couches in the library's open-air garden that overlooks Lady Bird Lake and downtown Austin. It's a relaxing place to browse a magazine or order a steaming drip coffee from the cart that dispenses beverages and pastries from the library's Cookbook Bar & Café.

Not many libraries grow their own garden, but that's just one of many novel ideas showcased at the $120 million, six-story, atrium-centered library. The building won a national award from the American Institute of Architects and the American Library Association and was cited by *Time* magazine as one of the nation's greatest new places in 2018. It's been described as the most daylight library in the nation.

Among its many sustainability features is a 373,000-gallon rooftop cistern that captures rainwater to supply the garden as well as restrooms. There's a parking garage beneath the building that includes space for 150 bicycles beside the Shoal Creek Hike and Bike Trail. Along with a collection of 500,000 books, there's a technology petting zoo that allows visitors to try out a 3D printer and other high-tech gadgets. The Cookbook Bar & Café serves foods prepared from the pages of cookbooks authored by local and touring cooks.

With a relaxing rooftop garden, coffee carts, and many other amenities, Austin's new Central Library is one of a kind.

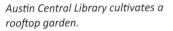
*Austin Central Library cultivates a
rooftop garden.*

If the rooftop garden inspires
you to do some planting of
your own, there's even a seed
library on the sixth floor where
visitors can check out seeds for
bluebonnets and scores of other
plants, sponsored by Central
Texas Seed Savers. The seeds are
checked out for the growing season and should be returned with
replacement seeds after the harvest.

LIBRARY WITH A VIEW

WHAT Austin Central Library

WHERE 710 W. Cesar Chavez St.

COST Free

PRO TIP Parking is also free
for the first 29 minutes in the
parking garage, but the garage
fills up early.

TALK THIS WAY, PLEASE

Why is Manchaca Road the most mispronounced name in Austin?

THIS ROAD DIDN'T GO ON FOREVER

WHAT Manchaca Road or Menchaca Road—take your pick.

WHERE Eight-mile road from Lamar Boulevard to Farm Road 1626

COST Free

PRO TIP The original Manchaca Springs isn't open to the public now, but it was a well-known landmark in frontier times, used as a stagecoach stop and watering hole on the road from Austin to San Antonio.

It's a little like that old joke about the puzzled traveler visiting Waxahachie, Texas for the first time. He pulled into a drive-in and begged the girl at the counter, "How in the world do you say the name of this place?" She looked at him pitifully and said as slowly as she could, "Dairy Queen."

For ages, strangers have been buzzing down Manchaca Road in South Austin without a clue about how locals pronounce it. Almost anyone who owns a business along the eight-mile street will proudly tell you, "Man-shack!"

That was all well and fine until city council members voted in 2018 to change the spelling of the name to Menchaca to honor the man they said it was originally named for, Jose Antonio Menchaca. He was a captain in the Texas Army who fought under Juan Seguin and Sam Houston at the Battle of San Jacinto that won Texas's

Manchaca Road may be the most mispronounced road, but Guadalupe Street that passes the University of Texas campus runs a close second. Locals call it "Guada-Loop," silencing the last syllable.

Left: The old name lives on in the titles of many businesses.

Bottom right: The most mispronounced road in Austin now has a new name, Menchaca.

independence. One legend holds that Menchaca camped in the area at Manchaca Springs. The name was misspelled by early settlers, who also misspelled Capt. Menchaca's name.

Business owners weren't happy about having to change all their signs and addresses, and some refused to change. They organized a group called "Leave Manchaca Alone" and contended that Menchaca didn't camp there. The name comes from a Choctaw word that might translate to "rear entrance," according to Marilyn McLeod, researcher and writer for the Manchaca-Onion Creek Historical Association. She said the name Manchac appears at several other landmarks the Choctaws traveled on their way from Louisiana through Texas. Some of the first Anglo travelers referred to it as "Manshack Springs." One called it "Manjack's Springs."

So it goes. The name change has encountered plenty of speed bumps, but perhaps it's possible to have it both ways. There is still an Old Manchaca Road that intersects with the new Menchaca Road.

AUSTIN'S LONG ROAD HOME

Why did it take Stephen F. Austin so long to get to Austin?

The Father of Texas didn't live long enough to enjoy the capital named in his honor. He did see Texas win its independence, but his own fortunes weren't going well. His rival Sam Houston trounced him (5,119 votes to 587) to win election as president of the new republic. In a conciliatory move, Houston appointed him secretary of state, but Austin died two months later. In frail health from the 14 months he spent in Mexican prisons, Austin succumbed to pneumonia in Columbia (now West Columbia) two days after Christmas in 1836. He was 43.

Houston said simply, "The Father of Texas is no more; the pioneer of the wilderness has departed." Austin never married or had children. He was buried at Peach Point, his sister's plantation near Brazoria where he often spent time. His body remained there for 74 years until his remains were moved to Austin for reburial at the Texas State Cemetery in 1910. A train brought him from Houston to Austin. A procession brought the coffin up Congress Avenue where it lay in state until burial the next day.

By that late date, only one of the pallbearers, W. P. Zuber, last survivor of the Battle of San Jacinto, had ever seen Austin in life. Austin was described by his private secretary as "...slender, sinewy and graceful—easy and elastic in his movements, with small hands and feet, dark hair which curled when damp, large hazel eyes, and in height about 5-foot-10 inches...his voice was soft, though manly."

One of his best-known likenesses is a portrait that hangs to the right of the speaker's desk in the Texas Senate. Austin is dressed in buckskin clothes, holding a long rifle. He is standing under a live oak with his spotted dog, Brand, beside him. It is a copy of an original destroyed in the 1881 fire at the old

A bronze statue of Stephen F. Austin stands tall in the Texas State Cemetery.

limestone capitol. The capitol also displays Elisabet Ney's marble statue of Austin. It stands on a pedestal that makes him as tall as the 6-foot-3 Houston, that Ney also sculpted.

Austin is also depicted in the bronze statue that marks his final resting place at the Texas State Cemetery. Welcome home, Stephen.

HONORING AUSTIN

WHAT Stephen F. Austin

WHERE Texas State Cemetery

COST Free

PRO TIP Audio tours, available weekdays from 8 a.m. to 5 p.m. at the visitors' center, highlight many of the heroes and famous Texans buried at the state cemetery; https://tspb.texas.gov/plan/tours/tours.html.

After Austin died, Sam Houston was among the first to call him the Father of Texas.

IT KEEPS ON TICKING

What clock still keeps time outside the little building that was once Austin's tallest?

Rancher, banker, and University of Texas (UT) benefactor George W. Littlefield enclosed the rooftop garden terrace of the Littlefield Building in 1913, making the nine-story building the tallest building in Austin and possibly the tallest building between New Orleans and San Francisco. The stout building on Congress and Sixth Street was home to American National Bank. Six large murals depicting scenes from Littlefield's ranches graced the lobby. The heavy bronze front doors, cast by the Tiffany Company, also featured bas-relief ranching scenes from his Yellow House Ranch. The cast iron, two-faced, clock sat out front.

The building remained Austin's tallest for 19 years until the Norwood Tower was built. It was a masculine setting, but the bank went out of its way to make women welcome, too. It featured a banking department set aside for the use of women who wanted to manage their own finances. As early benefactors of UT, Littlefield and his wife Alice also funded one of the first dormitories for women.

George Littlefield was left for dead on a Civil War battlefield. He survived and thrived and adopted the cattle brand, LFD, "Left for Dead." In addition to his mansion that's preserved on the University of Texas campus, he also funded the landmark Littlefield Fountain that helped anchor the university in Austin.

Littlefield was the university's biggest benefactor during its first 50 years. He had a long-running feud with another

Offices occupied part of the building. Lyndon Johnson was one of the tenants in 1935 when he worked for the National Youth Administration.

A big clock keeps good time outside the Littlefield Building.

LITTLEFIELD BUILDING

WHAT Littlefield Building and Littlefield Clock

WHERE 601 Congress Ave.

COST Free

PRO TIP This is a good spot to take a photo blending the old and new in downtown Austin.

philanthropist, George Washington Brackenridge, who hoped to see the campus move to a scenic, 500-acre tract of land along the Colorado River that he donated. Littlefield blocked the move to keep the campus on its original 40-acre site near downtown. He lived on the campus with Alice until time ran out on him at the age of 78 in 1920.

CLEARED TO LAND

How did the city's first airport become this neighborhood's runway to the future?

It's a little surprising to see an eight-story airport control tower standing in the middle of a residential area. But in the Mueller-planned development district, a lively place sprinkled with trendy shops and restaurants, the control tower is an old friend.

It's a tall reminder of Robert Mueller Airport, which closed in 1999, replaced by Austin-Bergstrom International Airport. The 700-acre airport site sat vacant for half a decade before it became the new home of the master-planned, mixed-use Mueller community. The mid-century modern tower, with distinctive blue and pale blue porcelain panels and a flared top, won an award from Progressive Architecture after it was competed in 1961 to direct flights at Austin's Mueller Airport. Then-Vice President Lyndon Johnson spoke at the dedication for the tower and a new terminal.

Just a few miles northeast of downtown, the airport outgrew its original site. Flight patterns brought jets over residential areas that grew up around it. Planes roaring low overhead on approach spooked motorists on nearby I-35. The closing of Bergstrom Air Force Base gave the fast-growing city the opportunity to move the airport to a more spacious location.

In 2018, the Austin Landmarks Commission voted to give landmark status to the tower. It has been proposed that the

The airport is long gone, but Mueller Airport Control Tower remains a popular landmark.

tower be restored and opened for tours. Lights adorn it during the Christmas holidays when the top still shines bright with the greeting, "NOEL."

One other airport landmark, the last wooden bow-trussed hangar in the country, now houses one of the city's most popular farmers markets on weekends.

END OF THE ROAD FOR GERALDINE

Why did the chicken cross Rainey Street?

The booming sounds of Austin music come from every corner of Rainey Street now. But long live the memory of Geraldine. She lived large and went out with a squawk.

Long before Rainey Street was a hip happening, Geraldine ruled the roost. She liked to take long leisurely strolls down the middle of the street. Sometimes she would just sit on the back dock of the Milagro café and chill. Or she would flap her wings, settle on a branch, and screech at strangers. She was the last of Rainey Street's guinea hens, the free-wheeling African chickens that once roamed the heavily Hispanic residential neighborhood near the convention center downtown. Big changes came after the area was rezoned as part of the central business district in 2004. One after another, bungalows built in the 1930s and earlier were converted into restaurants and bars with outdoor seating.

Geraldine (who actually turned out to be a male [Gerald?] when she was given a checkup by a veterinarian) continued to dodge cars, cabs, scooters, and bicycles. She/he took a final stroll on August 16, 2014. The end came suddenly when Geraldine was accidentally run over by a motorist. But she/he is still fondly

GERALDINE CHICKENED OUT

WHAT Rainey Street

WHERE The restaurant/bar at the Hotel Van Zandt, 605 Davis St., is named for a beloved chicken.

COST Hotel rates start at $300 a night.

PRO TIP Check out Geraldine the Rainey St. Guinea Fowl's Facebook page for other testimonials and memorial sites. "It's crazy how much we miss that darn bird," wrote one poster. "My favorite was when she chased people on Segway tours," another admirer posted.

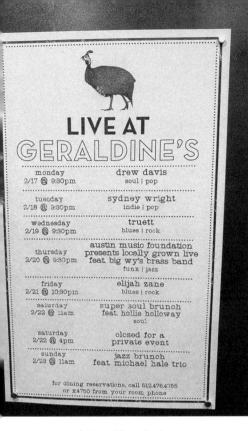

LIVE AT GERALDINE'S

monday 2/17 @ 9:30pm	drew davis soul | pop
tuesday 2/18 @ 9:30pm	sydney wright indie | pop
wednesday 2/19 @ 9:30pm	truett blues | rock
thursday 2/20 @ 9:30pm	austin music foundation presents locally grown live feat. big wy's brass band funk | jazz
friday 2/21 @ 10:30pm	elijah zane blues | rock
saturday 2/22 @ 11am	super soul brunch feat. hollie holloway soul
saturday 2/22 @ 4pm	closed for a private event
sunday 2/23 @ 11am	jazz brunch feat. michael hale trio

for dining reservations, call 512.476.4755
or x4750 from your room phone

In Loving Memory of **GERALDINE**

GERALDINE'S

Left: Geraldine, the last guinea to roam Rainey Street, is the namesake of a restaurant at posh Hotel Van Zandt.

Upper right: Geraldine was a free-ranging fowl, but memorials on Rainey Street mourn her loss.

remembered at several places around Rainey Street. The Royal Street Grocery features Geraldine's image, and her likeness adorns the front of a residential building next door. And the chic Hotel Van Zandt named its restaurant Geraldine in honor of the beloved bird. Live music plays there on stage most nights. You have to get there early to get a good seat. Just tell them Geraldine sent you.

Musician John Contreras sold the last private residence on Rainey Street in 2019 for $2.6 million.

SAINTED OIL

How did digging deep pay off for the University of Texas?

Frank Pickrell was fresh out of miracles. The primitive oil rig that sits today on the University of Texas campus had been pounding the dry Texas dirt for months without any luck. Pickrell climbed to the top of the derrick and took a handful of faded rose petals from a ragged envelope. He scattered them over the well. "I hereby christen thee Santa Rita," he whispered.

Santa Rita. Saint of the Impossible. It was what the Catholic women in New York who invested in his well told him to do. "These women became a little worried about the wisdom of their investment and consulted with their priest," Pickrell recalled. The priest was skeptical too. He blessed a rose in the name of Santa Rita. The women asked Pickrell to take it back to Texas with him, scatter the petals over the well, and call it Santa Rita. "I faithfully followed those instructions," the oilman said.

On May 28, 1923, nearly two years after the well was started, drillers heard a hissing sound they thought was a rattlesnake near the well bore. The hiss turned into a roar. A plume of oil gushed skyward past the top of the derrick and sprayed over the countryside for more than the length of two football fields.

The discovery well ushered in a new age of immense resources on public lands for the University of Texas and led the way for future discoveries in the vast Permian Basin.

In recognition of its importance to the school, the rig was moved from its original West Texas location in Big Lake to

MEET A MIRACLE

WHAT Santa Rita No. 1

WHERE Martin Luther King Boulevard at Trinity Street

COST Free

PRO TIP Parking around the UT campus is easiest at one of the university's 12 parking garages. Rates start at $4 for the first hour; parking.utexas.edu/parking/visitor.

The Santa Rita drilled the oil discovery that helped fund the University of Texas.

the Austin campus in 1940. Perhaps roses are still lucky for the Longhorns. They won their last national football championship in the Rose Bowl.

Santa Rita No. 1 played a part in the 2002 movie, *The Rookie*, which pictured a group of nuns scattering rose petals over the well. Dennis Quaid starred as a Big Lake high school teacher in his 30s who made it to the big leagues.

WHY THEY CALL IT "DIRTY'S"

What's the biggest change in almost a century at the city's oldest burger joint?

No more dirt floors. Those went away years ago. Other than that, you won't find any golden arches, drive-through lanes, or speaker boxes to order into. Martin's Kum-Bak has been cooking burgers the same way since it opened in 1926.

The street signs say Guadalupe, or "Guad-a-loop" as Texans say it, but its real name is The Drag, and it's been that way as long as anyone can remember. Plenty of other things have changed in Austin, the traffic, the music, the happening vibe downtown, but The Drag (short for Main Drag) holds on to one of the city's oldest dining icons, almost like a deified touchstone. The long, low white-painted restaurant hugs the edge of the street. Customers sit at tables near large windows that seem so close you could reach out and touch the passing cars.

John Martin opened the restaurant in the midst of the roaring '20s. The Drag became a lively hot spot which, by the '60s, morphed into a little bohemia, sprinkled with street people and panhandlers the students called "drag worms." There were ubiquitous eccentrics. One was Bicycle Annie, an elderly bicyclist who published her own newspaper and claimed, in 1948, to be the first woman to run for president. Her slogan: "It will take a woman to save America." The Drag changed more. It's a place where you could still sight some of the world's oldest hippies, but the street party moved on to other places, such as Sixth Street, Rainey Street, and anywhere else that turned up the music.

Opened in 1926, Martin's Kum-Bak is one of the oldest drive-ins in Texas.

The restaurant has had a front row seat on the street called "The Drag" for almost a century.

DIRTY'S ON THE DRAG

WHAT Martin's Kum-Bak

WHERE 2808 Guadalupe St.

COST $6.70 for a large Kum-Bak burger, $5.50 for a malt

PRO TIP Watch out for big crowds on game days.

But Martin's stayed true to its orange and white colors. Oh, there have been occasional changes. The original floors were dirt until they were paved with concrete in 1951. That's the reason many still call it Dirty Martin's. And in the '60s, owners knocked down the walls that originally separated it from the tavern next door and enlarged the dining room. Walls are covered with photographs of some of the most famous customers who often dine here, from legendary Texas football coaches to governors and well-known musicians.

You don't have to rub shoulders with anybody famous to enjoy a visit. Just take a seat by the window, order a Kum-Bak burger and a thick chocolate malt, and savor the moment.

YOU'RE GUILTY, BUT WE'LL NAME THE COURTHOUSE AFTER YOU

Was O. Henry innocent? The jury is still out.

It looked like the downcast defendant who sat in front of the jury at the stately federal courthouse on February 17, 1898, was all out of luck. He was fired from his job as a teller at the First National Bank of Austin. He liked to write, but the snappy little magazine he started had quickly failed. His beautiful young wife had died, leaving him with a little daughter to raise. Now he was charged with embezzling $854.08. He didn't even bother testifying in his own defense. After a brief trial, the jury pronounced him guilty. He was sentenced to five years in federal prison in Columbus, Ohio. It was a bitter end for William Sydney Porter. But it was just the start of something big for O. Henry.

The writer, who emerged from prison to become America's most acclaimed short story writer, is remembered at many landmarks his life touched during his youthful years in Austin. He was a draftsman at the Texas General Land Office, now the Texas Capitol Visitor Center. A licensed pharmacist, he helped fill orders at a drugstore on Sixth Street. With his beloved wife, Athol, he

---

Sympathetic visitors sometimes leave $1.87, often in pennies, on O. Henry's tombstone in Riverside Cemetery near Ashville, North Carolina, close to his birthplace. The tokens are from the opening of his short story, "The Gift of the Magi": "One dollar and eighty-seven cents. That was all. And sixty cents of it was in pennies." The change is gathered up quarterly and donated to local libraries.

Before he became O. Henry, William Sydney Porter went on trial in this building when it was a courthouse.

Inset: O. Henry's House is preserved as a museum. The writer kept his unsavory past a secret after he left Austin. The museum features photographs and memorabilia.

lived in the modest house that is now preserved as the O. Henry Museum at 409 E. Fifth St. Even the Renaissance Revival federal courthouse, which was recently elaborately renovated to its past glory, is now named O. Henry Hall. It was purchased by Texas State University for $8.2 million in 2015 for use as administrative offices. It was previously owned by the University of Texas, which renamed the building for the author. It is listed on the National Register of Historic Places. The US District Court for the Western District of Texas met there until 1936. The building was finished in 1879 under the supervision of Abner Cook, who also built the Texas Governor's Mansion.

There have been several failed efforts to gain presidential pardons for O. Henry, who is also one of the few felons to be honored with a US postage stamp. Some speculate that the three years he spent in prison (he was released early for good behavior) helped him focus and hone his craft as a short story writer. He went on to a prolific career in New York, publishing a story a week for newspapers. His early death at the age of 47 is said to have been brought on by years of heavy drinking.

A PUZZLING PICTURE

How many buildings can claim their own protest group?

The Independent, the tallest building in Austin, rises to a height of 683 feet with 58 floors. In a city that once had an ordinance that prohibited erecting any buildings taller than the Capitol, this one certainly overshadows the statehouse. Ground was broken in 2016, and the mixed-use project was completed in 2019.

Tenancy comes at a price—$400,000 to $5 million for residential units. The views are quite incredible, stretching far down I-35. Those who live here have access to a pool that is not for those with vertigo. It protrudes from the building in an angular fashion with an infinity-like edge, defying gravity as it hangs high over the city street. Built in the Seaholm District, an industrial area that was home to power and water treatment plants, its appearance mimics the look of the district. Inside the building, visitors will see a collection of artwork that breaks up tall stretches of industrial materials, concrete, and metal.

Not only is the Independent the tallest, it also has the most unusual nicknames. Its cantilevered structure gives it the appearance of a popular brain puzzler game, Jenga. Some call it Tetris after the game involving tile matching. Viewed from a distance, segments of floors in a block look like they were pulled out of formation over the block of floors below by an unseen giant hand. The building is topped by a steel fence that encloses a cylindrical object resembling a water tower. Critics of the design found fault with the top, or crown, and even started a protest group and a petition called, "Fix the Crown." However, there is a reason for the crown's unfinished look. Brett Rhode of Rhode

STANDING TALL

WHAT The Independent

WHERE 301 W. Ave.

COST Free

PRO TIP View this building from Auditorium Shores by the Stevie Ray Vaughan statue. Also, get a close-up from the Central Library in downtown Austin.

The unusual cantilevered design of the city's tallest skyscraper caused some critics to call it the Jenga Building. Photos courtesy of Sarah Thomas Randall.

Partners, the building's designer, explained that the top story's purpose is to offset winds that could make the building sway. Giant steel interlocking beams support the crown while the steel mesh enclosure allows air passage. Most importantly, the water tank, visible from the street, contains water that moves with the building, slowing the sway. Quite a feat.

Rhode said in response to the criticism, "Even the Eiffel Tower was hated. There was a huge move to tear it down." He is philosophical about the controversy caused by the structure, saying it is a great way to start talking about how the skyline might continue to develop.

The Independent is a new puzzle piece in the downtown skyline with a design that seeks to provide protection while taking advantage of beautiful vistas.

FOAM SWEET FOAM

Where is the oldest biergarten In America?

O. Henry enjoyed a cold one here. So have tens of thousands of Longhorn football fans.

August Scholz, a German immigrant, brought his entrepreneurial spirit and love of his native beer and food to the Hill Country when he opened Scholz Garten in 1866. The popularity of the early biergarten grew because of the presence of a large number of Prussian and Bavarian immigrants who appreciated the atmosphere and the abundant brews.

Visitors still gather for the camaraderie and reasonably priced imported German brew, starting at $5. German food is served in generous portions. Menu favorites include the Scholz schnitzel, a tasty pork loin dish for $16. A giant pretzel with a side of beer cheese ($10) is a great accompaniment for a cold stein of brew.

Listed on the National Register of Historic Places, Scholz's claims a long list of firsts, including the title of the oldest live music venue in the state. Another draw to Scholz's is that the live music during the week is free. Just one more example of Texas hospitality. The music

A COLD ONE AND AN OLD ONE

WHAT Scholz Garten

WHERE 1607 San Jacinto Blvd.

COST Brews start at $5 and wurst at $10.

PRO TIP This is the quintessential Longhorn football gameday party in Austin. Crowds pack the dining hall and biergarten.

In business for more than 150 years, Scholz Garten claims to be the oldest restaurant in Texas.

Scholz Garten has been hosting patrons for German food and beer since 1866.

still plays on, with local bands regularly entertaining. If you are a fan of Texas Longhorn football, you'll find like-minded people at this garden during football season. Be prepared to hear rousing choruses off "Hook 'em Horns" on game day. If you're in town for South by Southwest (SXSW), this is quite the welcoming gathering spot. Come in and raise a cold mug of beer at an outdoor table. It's a "Howdy" kind of place.

TURN ON THE MOONLIGHT

Where can you find the "party at the tower"?

People still search for the tower referenced in the movie *Dazed and Confused*. "Party at the moon tower," was the famous invite given by Matthew McConaughey's character in the film. That tower no longer exists. It is one of 16 original towers that have been extinguished forever, leaving the 15 remaining as the only such structures in the world.

Erected in 1894, standing 165 feet tall, the towers dotted the landscape of Austin for the precise purpose of banishing the darkness from Hill Country nights. Strong lights stood atop the towers, burning brightly with carbon arc bulbs. Geometric steel frameworks support the hooded lights that jut out from connected arms. The city chose these structures to illuminate the evening due to the very topography that gave the area its name. The hilly terrain made it impossible to rely on streetlights, similar to most cities of the era.

Tragedy has been associated with the historic high beams due to several people who have tried and failed to climb them. The tower at Guadalupe and Ninth is even said to be cursed due to reports of several murders perpetrated in the vicinity by a heinous ax slayer known as the Servant Girl Annihilator. *The Last of the Moonlight Towers* (2016) is a documentary detailing the history of the towers and their inclusion in the

The history of the city's distinctive Moonlight Towers is intertwined with the lore of serial killers and indie movies.

The nation's last Moonlight Towers still illuminate parts of the city.

National Register of Historic Places in 1970.

One of the towers shines brighter than all the others during the holidays. The tower in Zilker Park serves as the framework for the city's largest Christmas tree.

LUNAR LIGHTS

WHAT Moonlight Towers

WHERE Towers at Guadalupe and Ninth and Zilker Park are easily accessible.

COST Free. One can also view them on "Hop on and hop off" tours offered by Austin City and Hill Country Tours, $25 adults, $17 for children.

PRO TIP The towers have become such an integral part of Austin that they even inspired a retro rock band called Moonlight Towers, founded in 2001.

A CARNIVORE'S DELIGHT

Where can you find good barbecue if you're chomper challenged?

If tender beef and hundreds of loyal fans can save a landmark from laser-fast gentrification, Sam's BBQ has a chance.

The white-painted, wooden-sided restaurant has been operating on E. 12th for 63 years. Two owners have spanned those decades, claiming to serve the best hot sausage Austin has to offer. But the motto that gets the most attention is hand-lettered across the front of the building. "You don't need no teeth to eat my beef." And fans of the brisket attest to its "fall apart" tenderness. The restaurant is modest inside with historic photos on the walls and notes from loyal fans. An adjacent screened-in covered porch has tables and room to enjoy a meal and conversation.

Opened by Sam Campbell in 1957, the restaurant changed hands in 1976 when the Mays family purchased it. Great smoked meats and soulful music are hallmarks of the East Austin eatery. However, with the fluidity of the population, a new sound is heard in the capital city: the jingling of big money. The value of property has soared in East Austin, and condo developers have come knocking at Brian

KEEPING ON COOKING

WHAT Sam's BBQ

WHERE 2000 E. 12th St.

COST A brisket plate is $16.

PRO TIP Try a sausage wrap ($7) for a taste of the restaurant's famous hot sausage.

The owner wants to keep cooking barbecue, despite a reported $5 million offer from a developer to raze the restaurant.

In business since 1957, Sam's BBQ is holding on in rapidly gentrifying East Austin.

Mays' door with huge offers. The Mays family loves the business and the smell of a good brisket and have resisted. Brian prefers to ask his neighbors to support the BBQ restaurant and they have. Over the years, it's become a very diverse but still united neighborhood. Brian says, "The neighborhood is mixed now, so we've got to build our unity with who's here." But the jury is out. As the proprietor has said, "You've gotta go to Sam's while it's here because when it's gone, that's it."

NO LIMITS

What is the nation's longest-running televised music series?

Austin City Limits (ACL), created in 1974 by Bill Arhos, Bruce Scafe, and Paul Bosner, helped put the city on its way to becoming "The Live Music Capital of the World." Over the years, the series has received many accolades—National Medal of the Arts, Peabody Award, and induction into the Rock & Roll Hall of Fame. The show is recorded live and broadcast on KLRU of the Public Broadcasting Service (PBS).

Famous performers who have graced its stage include Willie Nelson, George Strait, Bonnie Raitt, Lyle Lovett, B. B. King, Gary Clark, Loretta Lynn, Ray Charles, Kris Kristofferson, Glen Campbell, and Hank Williams Jr., as well as many up-and-coming musicians. *ACL* has cemented its place in music history. The Rock & Roll Hall of Fame and Museum in Cleveland, Ohio, has digitally archived in its library almost 40 years of the show's footage. Visitors have access to more than 800 live performances of musicians who played on the iconic venue's stages.

The show has had several iterations, beginning with its first home in Communication Building B on the University of Texas campus. A venue with a seating of 300 made for an intimate experience each week. In 2011, *ACL* made the move

An offshoot of the TV series is the popular ACL Music Festival held at Zilker Park in October. Acts across the music spectrum appear at the six-day festival, which is divided into two weekends. Tickets begin at $265 for general admission.

Austin City Limits *moved to a spacious downtown music hall of its own in 2011 to accommodate more patrons.*

SHOWTIME

WHAT *Austin City Limits*

WHERE 210 W. 2nd St.

COST Prices vary depending on the show.

PRO TIP Performances for the PBS show run from late March through October. Find ticket information at www.acl-live.com or (512) 225-7999.

downtown to its own music hall in the Moody Theater in the Block 21 district, a large mixed-use development featuring shops, restaurants, and hotels. The downtown location provides more of an opportunity for residents and visitors to attend shows, with a larger capacity of 2,750 seats. Each season offers 18 to 20 live shows. The broadcast version on PBS runs approximately one hour.

GROCERIES FROM THE GOLDEN DAYS

Where do you go in Hyde Park when you need a great "sammich" and a basketful of memories?

Hyde Park exudes small-town charm. Lovely old homes dot the narrow streets with driveways full of bicycles and children's toys. This is a community where people know each other and keep an eye on everyone's children. Add to the mix a grocery store built in 1909 that looks as though it could be in a small Texas town wedged right between the post office and the railroad depot.

Avenue B Grocery and Market, the oldest continuously operating grocery in Austin, is a narrow wooden building with screen doors at its entrance. Even though it's a small place, you can find most staples you'll need. But the real treats are in the deli. The pimento cheese, a local favorite, is a heavenly homemade concoction. A deviled egg will set you back just 92 cents, but the sandwiches are the main act. The King Creole is hot and stuffed with deli meat and cheese. Vegetarian options are popular, led by the Queen B. Filled with cheese and the usual fresh fixins, it's made unique by the addition of smooth avocado, spicy jalapeño, and earthy mushrooms. Fresh bread choices abound with both light and dark rye, sourdough, white, and wheat, as well as gluten free.

AVENUE B GROCERY AND MARKET

WHAT 4403 Avenue B

WHERE 9 a.m. to 6 p.m. daily. Closed Sunday.

COST Sandwiches range from $4.25 to $9.50.

PRO TIP Take a gander at the old signage outside before you grab a picnic table and sample the pimento cheese.

Avenue B Grocery and Market, nestled in Hyde Park, is the city's oldest grocery and market.

It's your call. Pie and brownies are there for your sweet tooth. Grab a bag and shuffle along the weathered wooden floors to a place filled with friendly people lost in time.

A great sandwich or just a loaf of bread are staples at Avenue B Grocery and Market.

MOSAIC MYSTERY

Have you found your Magnificence today?

Come down to Congress Avenue. As you drive south, keep an eye out for eclectic shops, funky restaurants, and artwork hiding in plain sight. This is not your cool Austin vibe from the 2nd Street District, full of galleries, high-end clothing stores, and hot eateries. No, this is the part of Austin that brought about the catchphrase "Keep Austin Weird," coined by popular culturist Red Wassenich.

This is the South Congress (SOCO) energy that artist James Edward Talbot wanted to honor. Don't worry about missing this Austin landmark. It has its own little island, reigning over the xeriscape with its graceful, enveloping arms. People call this sculpture "it" due to the mystery of what it actually is. Is it alien or earthly? And that is just the confusion Talbot wanted from viewers. The one thing that Talbot wants people to take away from his work is that he believes that inside every person is inherent goodness. That is the message of this piece, installed in 2011 as part of the city's Art in Public Places project.

SOCO TREASURE HUNT

WHAT *Your Essential Magnificence* Sculpture

WHERE Intersection of 2204 S. Congress and 108 W. Live Oak St.

COST Free

PRO TIP See if you can locate the chair from the Broken Spoke that's incorporated in the sculpture.

As the architect behind his own eclectic personal residence Casa Neverlandia, Talbot brings the same philosophy to this commissioned artwork. He wants the audience to decipher its meaning for themselves.

James Talbot filled his roadside art with Austin relics.

To accomplish this work, Talbot worked in layers. First, he built the steel framework, adding concrete to create the body. The sculpture is covered with sparkling, colorful mosaics, which glisten in the sunlight. Hues of warm crimson flow into fuchsia and purple in the central eight-armed figure, framed by a ceramic aura of blues and greens. Surrounding this, the artist laid crushed tiles of yellows and golds, giving a richness and depth. A beautiful crescent sun acts as the crowning feature. The true Austin vibe of this piece comes from the addition of souvenirs from storied local venues: a chair from Broken Spoke dance hall (the seat in the sculpture), a frying pan from Nuevo Onda (bygone South Austin breakfast taco eatery), and a brick from Armadillo World Headquarters (now-demolished music venue from 1970-1980). All of these items, among others, lie buried in the work. A truly accessible piece, the sculpture and sculptor ask you to take a seat and become a part of the magnificence in your next photo.

MARGARITA WITH A VIEW

Where's the best place to watch a magnificent Texas sunset?

Theme restaurants spend a fortune creating atmosphere in order to beat the competition for food dollars. However, one restaurant has the win hands down. The Oasis, an outdoor extravaganza on Lake Travis, lays claim to a true star, the magnificence of a panoramic Texas sunset.

In 1982, entrepreneur Beau Theriot bought a 500-acre property high on a bluff above the lake. On it, he opened the aptly named Oasis, perched 450 feet above the water. The restaurant's draw truly depends on the scenery, so the construction of the seating area called for multiple levels for outdoor dining. Each level has an excellent view of the lake and the sunset. Reconstruction and additional building after a fire caused by an early morning lightning strike in 2005 helped the Oasis grow to become the largest outdoor restaurant in Texas. It covers 30,000 square feet. Approximately 2,500 patrons can be seated at one time.

The cuisine is Tex-Mex, with an emphasis on fajitas and burgers. Signature margaritas are a staple. Dining at the Oasis on a warm evening is like attending an outdoor wedding. You hear pleasant conversations all around you, but there is an atmosphere of heightened expectation as you await the arrival of the event's most important feature. When the sun starts to dip toward the

PARADISE ON THE CLIFF

WHAT The Oasis

WHERE 6510 Comanche Trl. Hours are 11:30 a.m. to 9 p.m. weekdays. 11:30 a.m. to 10 p.m. on weekends.

COST Specialty margarita, $8.75. Expect to spend $75 on dinner for two.

PRO TIP Get there early to get a front-row table. Big crowds show up for the nightly show.

Fantastic sunsets on Lake Travis helped the Oasis grow to become the largest outdoor restaurant in Texas.

horizon, creating a riot of red, gold, and purple hues, expect to hear loud applause. The sun winking goodbye as it disappears never fails to evoke awe in Oasis diners.

The largest outdoor restaurant in Texas has been enchanting diners for four decades with its multilevel front-row seat to nature's nightly show, the sunset.

CASA NEVERLANDIA

Where can you go in Austin for a Peter Pan experience?

Try James Talbot's constantly evolving residence, Casa Neverlandia. This architect and artist who has called Austin home for five decades purchased a South Austin bungalow in the '70s for $13,000. It was a very small, one-story structure, according to Talbot, calling for renovations that would make it the vibrant place it has become. A believer in sustainability and conservation, he avoids heating and air conditioning. His appliances are very energy efficient, and he pointed to a composting toilet in the backyard as evidence that he tries to give back to the environment. His energy and water usage are low, as he waters his yard with gray water from appliances. He prefers to dress accordingly, relying on clothing layers in winter and fans in summer. His reliance on natural light through large casement windows and reflective art in his home lessens his need for city wattage.

When you see Casa Neverlandia, you are struck by architectural features such as sharp peaks, rounded arches, colorful tiles and mosaics, and beautiful stained glass. Talbot's front yard has whimsical groupings of plastic ducks and plaster figures. The ducks, whose numbers continue to grow, are a reminder to watch low-hanging tree branches on the way up the steps inlaid with tiles.

Inside, the original one story has grown to three. The first floor is a work in progress, with its bump-out radiant heat fireplace and decorative altars dedicated to the elements: fire, air, water, and earth. The second floor, a gathering area with its chalet roof and bamboo-lined walls, is used for musical evening

This residence has evolved from a humble cottage to a multilevel unique abode, full of the artist's colorful works.

The architect and artist has turned his home into a house-sized work of art.

ARTIST'S DREAM

WHAT Casa Neverlandia

WHERE 305 W. Milton St.

COST Tours are by reservation on Talbot's website. $15 per person admission. For a tour, visit his Facebook page Casa Neverlandia, or contact him at www.talbot@talbotworld.com.

PRO TIP Be sure to visit Talbot's workshop to see the methods he uses to construct his art installations and his art pieces in his home.

events. Homage to places he has lived show up in Turkish rugs and Asian-themed altars. The top floor houses his bedroom, a jungle-themed affair, complete with a bathroom boasting a large bathing lagoon ensconced in sparkling blue tiles laid in waves. Don't call it a bathtub, he says. It transcends the ordinary bathroom experience.

Outdoors, visitors will find a backyard dedicated to xeriscape and workspace. If you're brave, you'll follow Talbot across a bridge suspended between the dwelling and a tree house. You must suspend your fear of heights. This, too, has three stages capped by a tower, upon which Talbot jokes, "You can see Dallas!" His creative process comes to fruition in his workshop, full of tools of the trade: bead looms, welding and heating equipment, tiles, and glass.

ROCK OF AGES

How sweet is that peace pie?

The sign in front of the pristine white wood church says, "Please join us. All are welcome." This house of worship has a long history of opening its doors wide. Clarksville residents, who were newly freed slaves, held religion in the highest regard as it allowed them ownership of the most important part of their lives. Because the community members were freed men and women, they valued their community and the dignity attached to it.

Now honored as a state historic landmark, the Sweet Home Missionary Baptist Church had humble origins, holding meetings in a nearby home. Finally, with $50 paid by the congregants, land was purchased on 11th Street. It was not an easy path nor a quick road to church establishment. The Clarksville residents were patient people. At first, members sang hymns and listened to the sermon under covering of a grove of trees. Several churches were finally constructed at the site, with the first being built in 1871. The third and current building was erected in 1935.

The church, which celebrates its 150th birthday in July 2021, still holds services on Sunday, with Bible study and choir practice during the week. Sweet Home continues to hold a "peace through pie" social on Dr. Martin Luther King Jr. Day. This event began in 2007 with a plethora of pies baked to raise funds for the church. Much like Costco, visitors get to sample the goods midweek and bid on the ones that tickle their fancy.

The small Baptist church continues traditions that began in Clarksville post-Civil War—the belief in freedom to practice one's religion.

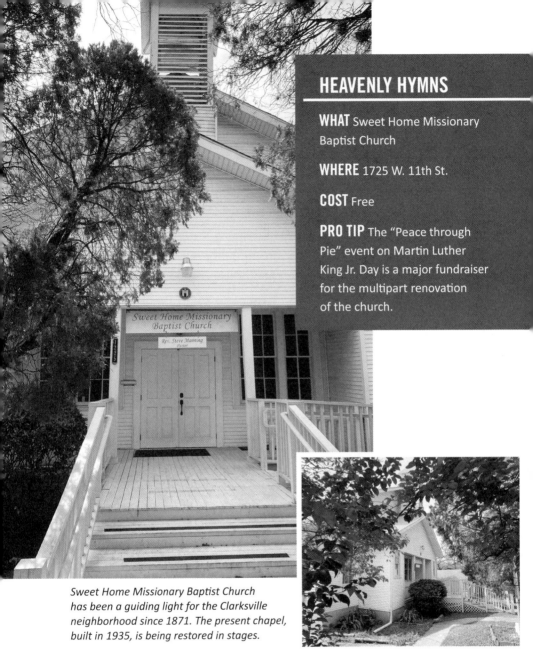

HEAVENLY HYMNS

WHAT Sweet Home Missionary Baptist Church

WHERE 1725 W. 11th St.

COST Free

PRO TIP The "Peace through Pie" event on Martin Luther King Jr. Day is a major fundraiser for the multipart renovation of the church.

Sweet Home Missionary Baptist Church has been a guiding light for the Clarksville neighborhood since 1871. The present chapel, built in 1935, is being restored in stages.

Sweet Home has been undergoing a major renovation that was started years ago by University of Texas engineering students who volunteered their time. It has since become a full-fledged plan to remedy the weakened foundation of the church, ensuring its viability as a place of worship for the community.

DOUBLE TROUBLE

How far can one musician's influence extend?

The tall bronze statue of musician Stevie Ray Vaughan blends two avenues of thought about the artist. The work, installed in 1993, stands on a pedestal on Auditorium Shores, next to Lady Bird Lake, which has served as the location of some of his concerts. Ralph Helmick, the sculptor, along with the musician's brother, Jimmie Vaughan, chose a meditative, calm posture for the singer who wears his hat low over his eyes and a poncho covering his shoulders. His guitar rests at his side. However, the additional bronze shadow lying behind Vaughan on his pedestal portrays the man playing his guitar.

Vaughan was a musician who hailed from Dallas but came to Austin, shaking up the music scene with his explosive combination of blues and rock. His vibrant, gritty music brought attention to the Austin music scene with tributes from David Bowie, Buddy Guy, and Robert Plant. Vaughan seemed quite drawn to elements of nature that could not be controlled. One of his early bands was Texas Storm. He gained renown for his rendition of "Texas Flood." Finally, his album *Couldn't Stand*

Stevie Ray Vaughan's talent brought him from the garage to the big stage.

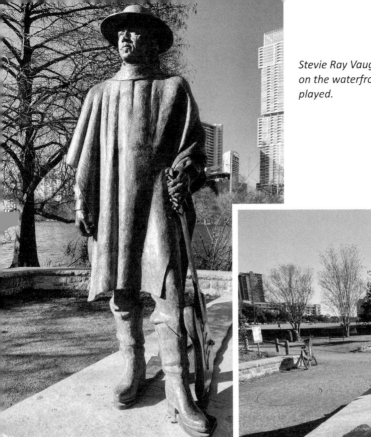

Stevie Ray Vaughan's statue stands on the waterfront near where he once played.

the Weather was highly praised and extremely successful. He died in 1990 in a helicopter crash after a performance. In 2015 he was inducted into the Rock and Roll Hall of Fame. This blues legend was well known for staying late to give autographs. He'd be pleased to know he's still here for his fans.

AN ALAMO SURVIVOR'S STORY

How did the Messenger of the Alamo end up in Austin?

It's just a simple, two-room house, but it gave Susanna Dickinson something she rarely ever had in her life—safety and security. She was a humble woman, who never learned to read or write. She signed her name with an "X." She was on her fifth marriage when she married Joseph Hannig, a German-born furniture maker who was 20 years her junior. They moved to Austin. Hannig built the "rubble rock" house in 1869 that sits now in Brush Square Park.

In Austin, Susanna began to put back together a life that had been unraveling since March 6, 1836. That was the day the Alamo fell. Susanna, then 21, huddled in the chapel with her two-year-old daughter, Angelina. In the midst of the battle, her first husband, Almaron Dickinson, rushed in. "My God, Sue, the Mexicans are inside our walls! If they spare you, save my child!"

She did. A day after the battle, she found Angelina sitting on Santa Anna's lap. He wanted to adopt her. Susanna refused. Santa Anna sent her off to spread the message of the Alamo to Sam Houston. In shock, she couldn't remember many details of the carnage. She wept for days.

In the years to come, Susanna would drift to many husbands and many places, New Orleans, Houston, and other stops. Then

---

MESSENGER OF THE ALAMO

WHAT Susanna Dickinson House Museum

WHERE 411 E. Fifth St.

COST Free

PRO TIP A cenotaph honors Susanna Dickinson at the Texas State Cemetery, but she is buried next to Joseph Hannig at Oakwood Cemetery.

Left: Susanna Dickinson settled into a happier life in Austin.

Top Right: In a life filled with sorrow, this little house brought Susanna Dickinson some happiness.

Bottom Right: A painting depicts Susanna Dickinson's exodus from the Alamo.

she found Hannig and Austin. They lived in the little house for six years and prospered, eventually moving to a bigger house in Hyde Park, where they stayed until her death in 1883. She was 68.

The house was moved in the early 2000s from a nearby location where it was used as a barbecue restaurant. Restored and furnished with family artifacts, it opened on Texas Independence Day, March 2, 2010, as part of a museum complex that includes the O. Henry House Museum and the Austin Fire Museum at Brush Square Park. It sits on one of the city's four original squares.

CHARLES UMLAUF'S SECRET GARDEN

Who was the professor who left Austin a priceless gift?

In a studio hidden on a wooded hillside at the edge of Zilker Park, Charles Umlauf spent a lifetime crafting his gift to the adopted city he loved. He was a struggling artist in Chicago when he was invited to teach life drawing and sculpture at the University of Texas in 1941. In 40 years of teaching before he retired as professor emeritus in 1981, Umlauf mentored hundreds of students, including many who went on to professional careers. One of them was Farrah Fawcett, who dreamed of becoming an artist before Hollywood sent her on a path to stardom. She and Umlauf remained lifelong friends.

All the time he was teaching, Umlauf continued to shape the sculptures that won him fame and slowly populated the spacious grounds of the parkside home he and his wife Angeline brought in 1944. In 1985, six years before his death, Charles and "Angie" donated their home, studio, and hundreds of sculptures to the City of Austin. Today, the Umlauf Sculpture

TREASURES IN A GARDEN

WHAT Umlauf Sculpture Garden and Museum

WHERE 605 Azie Morton Rd.

COST Adults, $7; seniors, $6; children 12 and under free.

PRO TIP Admission is free on Family Day with many special activities scheduled for children. Family Day is usually held on the second Sunday of the month, but dates sometimes vary. Contact the museum to confirm at (512) 445-5585.

Charles Umlauf's sculptures grace the Smithsonian, the Metropolitan Museum of Art, and the spacious garden he gave to Austin.

Charles Umlauf mentored hundreds of art students at the University of Texas and left the city a garden filled with a lifetime of sculptures.

Garden and Museum displays the artist's works on a relaxing and spacious six-acre site designed by landscape architect Aan Coleman, and an award-winning building designed by Lawrence Speck.

The sculptures that populate the grounds are wide and diverse. They range from whimsical animals to religious and mythological figures and sensuous nudes. There are bronzes and luminous marbles. When he couldn't afford marble, Umlauf poured a mixture of statuary cement and limestone aggregate into a mold to try to replicate it for one of his earliest sculptures, *War Mother 1939*, which was his response to the Nazi invasion of Poland. It brought accolades that caught the attention of members of the Art Department at the University of Texas, who invited him to teach. The Umlaufs returned the favor with their priceless gift, meant to be a thank you to the city that they loved.

THERE'S NO POOL LIKE AN OLD POOL

Where can you take a dip in the oldest swimming pool in Texas?

Barton Springs is more famous, but an even older pool in Austin has plenty of fans. Beside cold-flowing springs at the edge of the Colorado River, A. J. Eilers opened Deep Eddy Bathing Beach in 1915, three years ahead of the Barton Springs Pool, and early enough to lay claim to the title of oldest concrete swimming pool in Texas.

The Deep Eddy resort featured a Ferris wheel, a zip line across the Colorado River, a 50-foot-high diving tower, and a diving horse. The Deep Eddy Pool is a little more laid back than that now. It's a rectangle-shaped, family-friendly pool, chilled with 600,000 gallons of cool well water that is drained and refilled every other day. The temperature ranges from 65 to 75 degrees year round.

The city of Austin bought the pool in 1935, just before much of the resort was destroyed by a devastating flood. The city

WHERE STILL WATERS RUN DEEP

WHAT Deep Eddy Pool

WHERE 401 Deep Eddy Dr.

COST Adult nonresidents, $8; children nonresidents, $3.

PRO TIP Be sure to check out the mural wall that highlights diving horses, the "Human Fish," and other attractions that are part of the pool's colorful history dating back to 1915.

Country crooner Jimmie Dale Gilmore sang the praises of the pool and nearby Deep Eddy Cabaret in a 1989 song, "Deep Eddy Blues."

Deep Eddy Pool, the oldest in Texas, once had a diving platform for a horse.

Bottom inset: A mosaic mural traces the history of the pool that began as a spring-fed resort in 1915.

Mischievous teens known as the "Deep Eddy Rats" ruled the pool. Some performed unique and daring feats. Adventurous divers and a local man famous for sliding down the 50 foot slide in a precarious standing position added to the scene. Others, including "The Human Fish," were featured attractions. Acts created by locals were highly encouraged.

restored the pool, which was named for its location beside a giant boulder that formed an eddy in the river. The Works Progress Administration built the sturdy bath house in 1936 that is still used. Deep Eddy is on the National Register of Historic Places. The pool is also the namesake of several other enterprises, including the nearby Deep Eddy Cabaret, a bar opened in 1951, and the Deep Eddy Vodka distillery.

MUSIC FOR A GENERAL ON MOUNT BONNELL

What famous general brought a band with him when he climbed Austin's favorite overlook?

Most visitors come to Mount Bonnell to look. The ill-fated George Armstrong Custer and his wife Libbie went there to listen.

Many legends hover over the 775-foot tall landmark that overlooks Lake Austin and the surrounding hills. Frontiersman "Big Foot" Wallace killed bears there—and Indians. Daredevil Hazel Keys slid down a cable to the riverbank in 1898. Her trained monkey, smart for his size, went second. But few past visits echo more loudly than the picnics the Custers had there when they lived in Austin just after the Civil War.

The trail to the top was a little too steep for cavalry horses, the celebrated general noted. He and Libbie had to walk. They brought the 6th Cavalry regimental band with them. Their favorite song? "The Anvil Chorus." Custer said the "sound descended through the valley grandly." And you think the music in Austin is loud now.

Mount Bonnell's 600-foot upthrust is one of the tallest natural faults in the Balcones Fault formation. It's said that Spanish explorers thought the tall cliffs resembled balconies. It takes about 10 minutes to climb the 100 steep steps to the top. It takes your breath away—so do the spectacular vistas of Lake Austin, the surrounding hills, and, on a clear day, downtown Austin. It's also a prime place for watching fireworks on the Fourth of July.

MUSIC ON THE MOUNTAIN

WHAT Mount Bonnell at Covert Park

WHERE 3800 Mount Bonnell Dr.

COST Free

PRO TIP Bring a snack. It's a popular spot for a picnic, so get there early. Tables are limited at the top.

Bonnell offers a panoramic overlook of Lake Austin and the Hill Country.

Another romantic legend holds that the first time a couple visits Mount Bonnell, they will fall in love. The second time they will get engaged, and the third time they will marry.

THE QUEEN OF ORATORY

What soft-spoken leader spent her life blazing new trails for African American women in America?

Travel to Austin-Bergstrom International Airport (ABIA). You'll be greeted by a larger-than-life bronze statue of Barbara Jordan, installed in 2002. In the terminal named after her, the artwork by sculptor Bruce Wolfe shows the legislator/professor seated in a large chair in a contemplative pose. A scholarly and thoughtful woman, her fingers touch tent-like in front of her face. In her lap lies an opened book covered by her ever-present glasses. Barbara Jordan (1936-1996) cast a giant shadow over the city of Austin. A native of Houston, this lawyer, Texas legislator, and US congresswoman, changed the shape of politics for the nation and for women.

A member of the House Judiciary Committee during the Watergate hearings, she gave an impassioned speech on the House floor at the beginning of the Nixon impeachment hearings. Her mellifluous voice and stunning oratorical gifts brought her to national prominence. Sometimes you just wish a statue could talk.

TEXAS ICON

WHAT Barbara Jordan statue

WHERE University of Texas statue at 307 W. 24th St. and ground floor at Austin-Bergstrom International Airport

COST Free

PRO TIP This statue came to be because of the efforts of a UT service group known as Orange Jackets who worked in concert with other student groups to pass a referendum in 2003 to dedicate $1 in student semester fees to the statue project.

After she left politics, Barbara Jordan served as a professor at the University of Texas/LBJ School of Public Affairs.

Barbara Jordan's statue at the Battle Oaks grove of trees was the first statue of a woman on the University of Texas campus.

Her many firsts included being the first African American woman elected to Congress from a Southern state and the first to give the keynote address at a presidential convention (Carter in 1976 and Clinton in 1992).

After her political career, Jordan accepted a position as a professor at the University of Texas/LBJ School of Public Affairs, ensuring her continuing influence as an educator. For 16 years, she was a part of the Austin education community. Her second statue, also by Bruce Wolfe, was erected in 2009 at the Battle Oaks grove of trees near the Texas Union. This bronze, the first statue of a woman erected on the UT campus, portrays Ms. Jordan as the serious person she was. Her hands rest on her waist in much the same posture as every teacher who has ever had to counsel a student. She remains vigilant.

HANK'S LAST SHOW

What really happened to Hank Williams when he performed his last show at the Skyline Club in Austin?

By most accounts, Hank Williams put on an amazing show when he hit the stage of the Skyline Club on a Friday night, December 19, 1952. He was dressed in a white suit with a crisp white hat. A thousand people crowded into the low-slung honky-tonk that usually held a couple hundred. Club owner Warren Stark drove down with the country crooner from Dallas in Hank's Cadillac. Hank, by then, was famous for his "no shows" or sometimes passing out on stage when he did show up. In Dallas at an earlier show, it's said a club owner still charged fans to see their hero unconscious backstage. Stark wanted to make sure Hank kept his date in Austin. They say he sang for three hours. Hits like "I'm So Lonesome I Could Die," and "Your Cheating Heart." He even performed a few gospel songs.

One of the house band members who backed up Hank remembered it a different way. Jim Grabowske, a steel guitar player, recalled that Hank struggled and had to stop midway through his second set. An ambulance had to be summoned and Hank was taken to Brackenridge Hospital to be treated for

Elvis headlined a show at the Skyline on October 6, 1955. He was a regular on the *Louisiana Hayride* show, as were Hank and Johnny Horton. Two months before Hank came to Austin, he and 19-year-old Billie Jean Jones were married at New Orleans Municipal Auditorium. They sold tickets. The ceremony was performed twice. Fourteen thousand people attended.

A CVS drugstore stands on the site of the Skyline Club.

Inset: Hank took the stage for his last concert in Austin. Photo from Pictorial Press, LTD/ Alamy Stock Photo

what possibly was a heart attack. The crowd didn't know, Grabowske said, because Hank was taken out the back. He said his Cadillac sat outside the club for days afterward.

Whether Hank was stricken ill that night or not, the concert at the Skyline was his last. Hank died 11 days later in the back seat of a Cadillac while he was being driven to a New Year's show in Canton, Ohio. A coroner's jury ruled he died of a severe heart condition and hemorrhage. He was 29.

Out on far North Lamar Boulevard, which was better known as the Dallas Highway, the Skyline's neon sign kept on welcoming music fans until the 1970s. After it closed, another music hall, Soap Creek Saloon, occupied the 10,000-square-foot building with a low ceiling and a crowded, low-slung stage barely higher than the dance floor. It was razed in 1989 to make way for the widening of North Lamar and Braker Lane. A CVS drugstore was built on the site. Austin was burgeoning toward the north, but even then, you couldn't see the skyline like the neon promised.

THE FLOOD THAT LIFTED UP WHOLE FOODS

How did a flood change the fate of a fledging health food store?

Just four blocks from the massive market that holds the company's world headquarters, a thrift store occupies the site where the first Whole Foods Market almost went down with the ship.

Cofounders John Mackey and Renee Lawson faced plenty of hurdles when they started their modest, 11,000-square-foot health food store in downtown Austin. But nothing hit harder than the devastating Memorial Day flood that almost swept it away in 1980. Eight feet of water swirled inside, ruining everything. They had no insurance.

What happened next floored them. Everyone came to the aid of the store—employees, vendors, customers, and even total strangers. They worked day and night to get it reopened in 28 days. One customer told Mackey she didn't want to live in a city that didn't have a store like Whole Foods.

The company survived and thrived, merging or buying out other health food stores around the nation. It was purchased by Amazon in 2017. It had 500 stores in 2019.

Goodwill Industries of Central Texas opened a thrift store and donation center on the site of the first store in 2014. The following year it flooded on the same date that the Whole

Cofounders John Mackey and Renee Lawson had to live in their first store when a landlord kicked them out of their duplex for warehousing food inside.

DRY GROCER

WHAT Site of Whole Foods Market's first store

WHERE 914 N. Lamar Blvd.

PRO TIP Now on high ground, the top-floor terrace at the headquarters store turns into an ice-skating rink during the Christmas holidays.

Top: The original location of the store that became Whole Foods Market is now home to a thrift store.

Inset: An ATX sign stands in front of Whole Foods headquarters.

Foods Market flooded 34 years earlier. This time, Whole Foods stepped in to help with zero interest loans and other aid. An old debt kindly repaid.

HOW THE STATE FLOWER LOST ITS THORNS

How did a painting help plant the seeds of millions of bluebonnets?

Prickly pear cactus might line the roadways of Texas if history had taken a wrong turn, but the Texas legislature was swayed to pick a different flower in 1901. For that, you can thank the bright still life *Bluebonnets and Evening Primrose* that Austin artist Mode Walker captured on canvas a year earlier. It greets visitors to the Neill-Cochran House Museum, headquarters for the Texas branch of the National Society of the Colonial Dames of America.

Powerful orators argued mightily for the state to choose other flowers. John Nance Garner, a future US vice president, spoke passionately about prickly pear blossoms. He considered them as beautiful as orchids.

The Colonial Dames marched themselves into the heart of the debate. They put vases of fragrant bluebonnets on the desks of all the legislators. And they brought along Mode's painting because in those days not everyone was certain what a bluebonnet looked like.

Gov. Joseph D. Sayers signed the law making it the state flower on March 7, 1901, just in time for wildflower season.

John Nance Garner's love for prickly pears stuck with him. He was known forever more as "Cactus Jack."

The Neil-Cochran House is considered to be one of the most significant 19th-century historic residences in Austin. During its

---

BELOVED BLOSSOM

WHAT Neill-Cochran House Museum

WHERE 2310 San Gabriel St.

COST Guided tours for adults, $12; seniors, $10; children under 12, free.

PRO TIP Guided tours give visitors an up-close view of this often-overlooked landmark.

Top: Mode Walker's painting helped convince the legislature to make the bluebonnet the state flower.

Inset: Abner Cook, builder of the Governor's Mansion, also designed the landmark Neill-Cochran House, where Walker's painting now hangs.

early years, it served as the state's first school for the blind and was also used as a hospital for federal troops during Reconstruction. The museum also preserves on its grounds what is thought to be the city's only surviving slave quarters. Enslaved Blacks comprised 28 percent of the city's population at the start of the Civil War in 1861. New interpretive programs and research at the house museum focus on the work that enslaved people played in the building of the city and what life was like for them in that period.

While the original bill only included one variety of bluebonnets, the legislature amended the law in 1971 to include all the other varieties found in the state.

BE WARY OF HAIRY

If the county cuts down the trees, where will the Hairy Man hide?

A long time before there were any barber shops in the Austin area, the Hairy Man grew into a shaggy legend. They say he was just a boy when he was separated from his parents' wagon train along Brushy Creek in Round Rock in the 1800s. It isn't clear how he was lost. Some say he fell off the wagon. Others believe he was carried away by the flooding creek. Either way, the boy was left alone to become a hermit in the wilderness. He grew into a Hairy Man. And he didn't like strangers.

He liked to scare away travelers on the trail that ran along Brushy Creek. Sometimes he would just yell and wave his arms. Other times he would climb up into the limbs of the tall oak trees that formed a canopy over the road. He would drag his feet along the roofs of stagecoaches and terrify passengers. That's how Hairy Man met his fate. He fell in front of the horses of a passing coach and was trampled.

But they say that on dark nights, the ghost of Hairy Man still leaps out from his hiding places in the woods. There have been numerous sightings. The Round Rock Parks and Recreation Department posted a photograph of an extremely large footprint on its Facebook page. The lane along Brushy Creek

HAIRY AND SCARY

WHAT Hairy Man Road

WHERE Narrow tree-canopied drive along Brushy Creek

PRO TIP Hairy Man Festival is usually held on the Saturday closest to Halloween at Cat Hollow Park, sponsored by the Brushy Creek Municipal Utility District; www.bcmud.org.

Not many monsters have a road named after them, but this one does.

One of the rare roads named for a monster winds through the trees.

is named in his honor, Hairy Man Road. There's also a Hairy Man Festival each October. It includes a 5K run on Hairy Man Road and a Hairy Man look-alike contest.

Locals seemed to live in harmony with the monster until 2019 when county commissioners proposed to cut down trees and widen Hairy Man Road. That raised the hair on the necks of area residents. They gathered more than 20,000 signatures online to protest the tree cutting. The debate continues, but a compromise was offered to cut fewer trees. Safety is an issue. The road is narrow. Motorists drive too fast—not out of fear of Hairy Man— they're just in a hurry.

A WINDOW ON THE WORLD

What famed architect designed his first church in Austin?

St. Mary's Cathedral has been a huge part of the Austin religious community since its first iteration. The first church was called St. Patrick's and was constructed in the 1850s, one block north of its home today. The choice to rename came about as a compromise between two groups of parishioners, Irish and German immigrants, both very important communities in the early days of the city. Both groups found naming the church after St. Mary very acceptable.

CHERISHED CHURCH

WHAT St. Mary's Cathedral

WHERE 203 E. 10th St.

COST Free

PRO TIP View the famous Rose Window from both the street and inside the sanctuary.

The cathedral was designed by Irish architect Nicholas Clayton, an interesting choice in that he had never designed a church. His experience with St. Mary's was auspicious, setting him on the path of building many other celebrated works, such as the Main Building at St. Edward's University.

A mighty bell, weighing a full ton, was donated by the family of Michael Butler, an Irish immigrant who came to Austin and created a successful brickmaking business. His grandchildren's names are engraved on the bell. The windows in St. Mary's are among its most stunning features. They were purchased

St. Mary's Cathedral, one of the city's oldest churches, is a landmark designed by Nicholas Clayton.

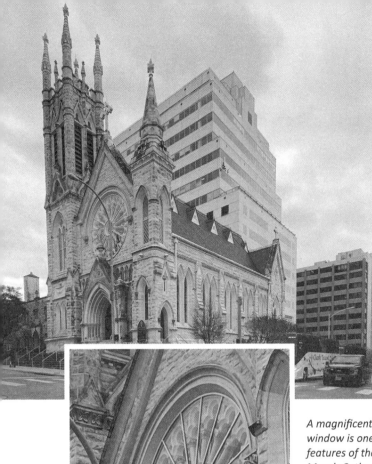

A magnificent stained glass rose window is one of the crowning features of the landmark St. Mary's Cathedral.

from a firm in France and installed in 1890. The Rose Window is of interest for its size and intricacy. Once hidden behind organ pipes, it is now in full view. The term "Rose" refers to a design that blossoms with numerous petals radiating from a circle. The patterns are intricate and colorful.

Plants and flowers of the Hill Country are featured in wooden panels, installed around and over the altar during a later renovation. There are carved images of cacti and bluebonnets.

COMEDY MEETS MAGIC

Do you want to be in Show Biz?

Walking down Sixth Street on a cool spring evening, you'll notice several folks pull up short outside a large storefront window, waving, ogling, and posturing for an appreciative audience. Those windows are the eyes into the crazy world of Esther's Follies. This revue birthed from creative bits and pieces of Austin's early entertainment scene featuring comedy, mimes, magicians, illusionists, satirists, dancing, and singing.

It started as an amateur event at a small bar on Sixth Street, bringing out local talent who performed around a water sprinkler under an awning. Making this creative hodgepodge a tribute to the Olympic swimmer and actress Esther Williams seemed like a great idea. The creative forces behind this addition to Austin's entertainment scene in 1977 were Michael Shelton and Shannon Sedwick, University of Texas alumni and husband and wife. Shelton is the designer of Esther's venue. Shannon ramrods the troupe of performers while she brings to life icons such as Patsy Cline and Governor Ann Richards.

Housed in a brightly painted corner building covered with art celebrating the aquatic life, the Follies have survived and thrived for more than 40 years. Magic is a huge part of any Esther's evening. Ray Anderson is an award-winning magician with almost four decades as a Follies' regular. You can expect to see him zip line into the theater before he levitates assistants in outrageous skits.

During those decades, the cast at Esther's has skewered the high and mighty. If you're in the *Austin American-Statesman* headlines, you'll probably end up the subject of a comedy sketch or a raucous song. Likewise, politicians in the national arena will find themselves parodied as well. Some of the funniest moments occur when the cast selects an audience member to participate. If you sit up front, you're a likely target. Volunteers and cast don't keep all the humorous shenanigans inside. A hidden door at the back of the stage allows the show to use the street as a part

Esther's Follies has been making audiences laugh at its zany theater on Sixth Street since 1977.

of the hijinks. Outside the large windows, suddenly a boat might float by in its prop waves. Dummies replace actors and are sent flying high in the night sky. You just never know what Michael Shelton will dream up.

It's all in good fun and shows no sign of slowing down.

FUN AND FRIVOLITY

WHAT Esther's Follies

WHERE 525 E. Sixth St.

COST Ticket prices online begin at $30.

HOURS Shows are at 8 p.m. and 10 p.m. Thursday through Sunday.

PRO TIP On a weekend evening, head to Esther's front window to put yourself in a comedy sketch.

A theater that started on a whim has grown into one of the nation's longest-running comedy shows, on stage for more than 40 years.

CHIPS OFF THE OLD BLOCK

What is the city's stateliest street?

John and Eugene Bremond, two entrepreneurial brothers, used a city block to create a row of elegant homes. These were built for their family and have been christened the Bremond Block. These 11 houses were erected in a period stretching from 1850 to 1910 and pay homage to architectural styles ranging from Victorian to Greek Revival. The homes all made use of indigenous building materials such as local brick and stone. All are included in the National Register of Historic Places.

Houses that are high points include the John Bremond, Jr home at 700 Guadalupe St., built in 1886 by George Fiegel. The cast iron porch that wraps around the first floor is enclosed by ornate grill work. The second floor mirrors the first with a balcony that stretches across the home, bearing the same intricate iron grill work. The Victorian design of the house is enhanced with its arches, dormers, and gables. The mansard roof has slate shingles. This building has been used by its owner, the Texas Classroom Teachers Association (TCTA), as offices.

STREET OF STYLE

WHAT Bremond Block

WHERE 700 Guadalupe St. to 900 San Antonio St.

COST Free. However, houses are not open to the public.

PRO TIP These houses can be viewed on a self-directed tour.

The Bremond Block is a showcase of elegant 19th-century architecture. Enjoy a step back in time with some of Austin's most beautiful architectural jewels.

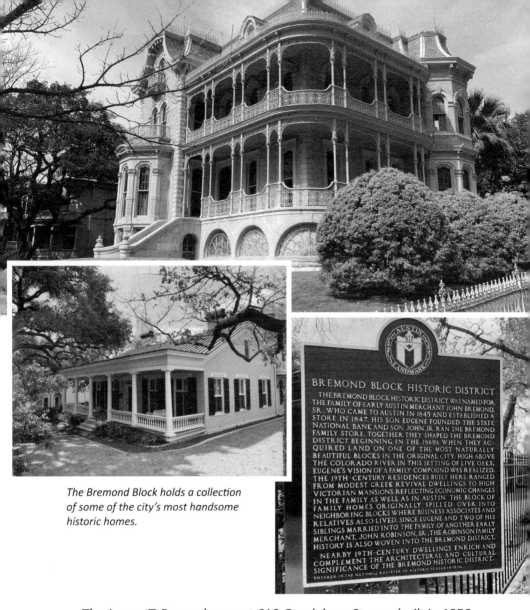

The Bremond Block holds a collection of some of the city's most handsome historic homes.

BREMOND BLOCK HISTORIC DISTRICT
THE BREMOND BLOCK HISTORIC DISTRICT WAS NAMED FOR THE FAMILY OF EARLY AUSTIN MERCHANT JOHN BREMOND, SR., WHO CAME TO AUSTIN IN 1845 AND ESTABLISHED A STORE IN 1847. HIS SON EUGENE FOUNDED THE STATE NATIONAL BANK AND SON JOHN JR. RAN THE BREMOND FAMILY STORE. TOGETHER THEY SHAPED THE BREMOND DISTRICT BEGINNING IN THE 1860s WHEN THEY AC-QUIRED LAND ON ONE OF THE MOST NATURALLY BEAUTIFUL BLOCKS IN THE ORIGINAL CITY. HIGH ABOVE THE COLORADO RIVER IN THIS SETTING OF LIVE OAKS, EUGENE'S VISION OF A FAMILY COMPOUND WAS REALIZED. THE 19TH-CENTURY RESIDENCES BUILT HERE RANGED FROM MODEST GREEK REVIVAL DWELLINGS TO HIGH VICTORIAN MANSIONS, REFLECTING ECONOMIC CHANGES IN THE FAMILY AS WELL AS IN AUSTIN. THE BLOCK OF FAMILY HOMES ORIGINALLY SPILLED OVER INTO NEIGHBORING BLOCKS WHERE BUSINESS ASSOCIATES AND RELATIVES ALSO LIVED. SINCE EUGENE AND TWO OF HIS SIBLINGS MARRIED INTO THE FAMILY OF ANOTHER EARLY MERCHANT, JOHN ROBINSON, SR., THE ROBINSON FAMILY HISTORY IS ALSO WOVEN INTO THE BREMOND DISTRICT.
NEARBY 19TH-CENTURY DWELLINGS ENRICH AND COMPLEMENT THE ARCHITECTURAL AND CULTURAL SIGNIFICANCE OF THE BREMOND HISTORIC DISTRICT.
ENTERED IN THE NATIONAL REGISTER OF HISTORIC PLACES IN 1970.

The James T. Brown home at 610 Guadalupe St. was built in 1858. A Greek Revival structure, it is less imposing than the Bremond residence. The one-story residence features Greek columns across its front elevation, framing its porch.

The Pierre Bremond house built in 1898 sits on a lot surrounded by artfully designed iron fencing at 402 W. Seventh St. This Victorian example has a tower, bow windows, a porch with iron grillwork, and a similarly designed upper balcony. The exterior is a light brown brick made in Austin. This structure is also owned by TCTA.

HEAVEN FOR FOODIES

Where can you find a good rolling restaurant?

Austin is a casual city that likes its food spicy, its coffee strong, and its cuisine multicultural. While brick-and-mortar restaurants are a big part of the economic lifeblood of the city, residents have a new favorite; the cafe on wheels. Small trucks selling authentic tacos at construction sites have turned into airstream trailers with built-in kitchens serving up Korean barbecue, Thai entrees, Lebanese specialties, and Louisiana creole cooking. Instead of being scattered across the city, they now have trailer parks for customers who value variety, cost, and speedy service. Looking at the menus, visitors will find food choices once reserved for the state fair, such as chicken, shrimp, or avocado in a cone.

Ubiquitous food trucks such as hot dog and hamburger vendors are still a big part of the new wave, but an ability to provide more options has drawn in diners. Burgers have graduated to tzatziki dressing with a fried egg on top for good measure. When you visit a food truck park, you'll find a multicourse meal if you wish. Juice trucks whet your whistle. Savory specialties such as wurst, gyros, and lobster rolls compete for your dollar. Dessert is not far behind, with ice cream and gelato for a hot day.

The city is home to approximately 1,000 mobile food vendors. Those in parks have found a way to cater to everyone's needs.

Where else can you find freshly made authentic gnocchi, fried pickles, and a haircut with a side of live music? And, if you're feeling stressed out, how about a yoga session? And children are welcome too. This has become the new wave in laid-back

Whether you want a down-home burger with a fried egg or a tasty authentic plate of gnocchi, hundreds of food trailers can satisfy your cravings.

Austin is home to more than 1,000 food trailers that supply the city with a movable feast.

CHEFS ON WHEELS

WHAT Food trailers

WHERE 7800 S. First St. and 1720 Barton Springs Rd.

COST $5 to $16

PRO TIP The dining is alfresco, so be prepared for the possibility of rain.

dining. Everyone gets what they want to eat while they enjoy lunch on a shady bench.

The Thicket Food Park, 7800 S. First St., a collection of food and service trucks, has become a part of the South Austin community since its start in 2015. It's a place for families. There is even a community garden. Bring your neighbors, your kids, and your dogs. Playscapes greet children, and picnic tables in the shade provide comfort and friendly company. Adam Diaz opened this park with the idea of providing a welcoming venue with good food, fun music, activities for families, and a good haircut if you find yourself looking a bit shaggy.

The Picnic at 1720 Barton Springs Rd. is the original food park, with its nod to many world-famous cuisines. A centrally located venue, it offers the creature comforts of restrooms, pavilions, and great local food.

A ROCKY RECEPTION

How did Austin's neighboring suburb pick its name?

Sometimes the best choice is sitting right in front of you. Round Rock came to be because of cattle drives and other early trails that made it a popular river crossing on Brushy Creek. Cattle drovers used the Chisholm Trail to push their herds from the Rio Grande River to the railroads of Abilene, Kansas. Water crossings posed a real danger. Brushy Creek, the local body of water, could be dangerous when the water rose. The creek was also the original name of the community. In it sat a large, flat, anvil-shaped limestone rock that cowhands used as a marker to know when the river was low and the crossing was safe. It wasn't a stretch to call it a round rock. Cattle, wagons, and riders headed for that boulder. They left wheel ruts in the creek bed that remain.

Two residents liked to fish from that same rock. Jacob Harrell, an Austin blacksmith, and Thomas C. Oatts, postmaster, knew that lucky fishing place quite well. When postal system administrators called for a new name for the town, the two suggested Round Rock. The name was confirmed on August 24, 1854.

The namesake rock still is a pleasant place to cross the river on Chisholm Trail Road, a historic drive just west of the interstate. A

ROCKY ROAD

WHAT The real round rock in Round Rock

WHERE Memorial Park, 600 N. Lee St.

COST Free

PRO TIP Nearby Memorial Park features bronze sculptures that honor pioneers and other trailblazers, and it's a pleasant place for a picnic.

One of the best-known landmarks from the Chisholm Trail is still solid as a rock.

Top: A round rock marked a safe crossing for cattle herds and others.

Inset: Sculptures in Memorial Park pay tribute to the hardy pioneers and longhorns who passed this way.

nearby waterfall, manmade, offers a soothing backdrop for a picnic lunch. Beside the crossing, Memorial Park honors the settlers and cattle drovers who passed this way. Bronze statues of longhorns were created by Jim Thomas, a renowned western artist. The *Bell Steer* is dedicated to the animal who wears a bell and leads the herd. If a driver wanted to find the head of the herd, he would listen for the bell. Other sculptures by Thomas include *The Pioneer Woman*, dedicated to Hattie Cluck, a local settler who was in the vanguard of female pioneers. She is said to be the first woman to travel the Chisholm Trail. Facing her, another sculpture named *The Pioneer Boy* is dedicated to her five-year-old son, Emmett Cluck, who traveled the trail with her.

TALK THIS WAY, PLEASE (page 22)

THE INDEPENDENT (page 38)

SWEET HOME MISSIONARY BAPTIST CHURCH (page 56)

CHARLES UMLAUF SECRET GARDEN (page 62)

SPARKY PARK (page 106)

BREMOND BLOCK (page 82)

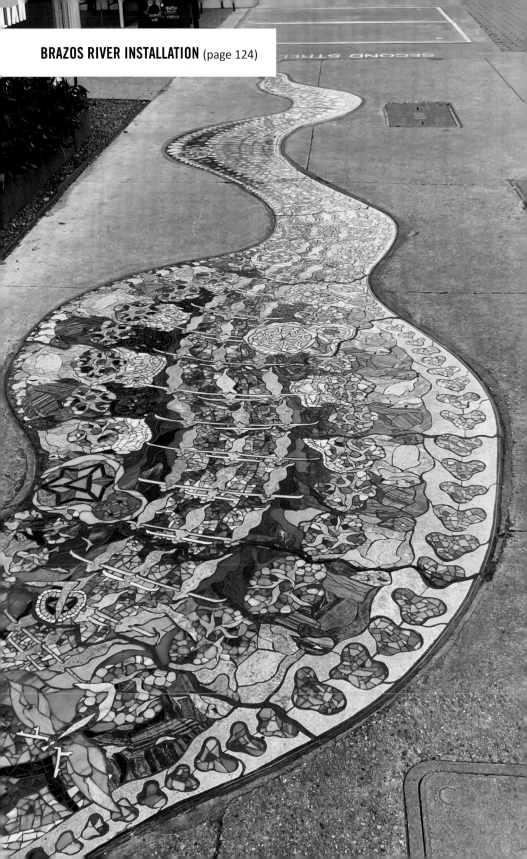

MONOCHROME FOR AUSTIN (page 142)

FORMER WORLD HEADQUARTERS OF AMERICAN ATHIESTS (page 172)

BLANTON MUSEUM OF ART (page 184)

DRISKILL HOTEL (page 132)

BROKEN SPOKE (page 108)

ST. EDWARD'S HILLTOPPERS (page 150)

REDDY KILOWATT WOULD BE PROUD

What is hiding in plain sight in Sparky Park?

What do you do when you have an electrical substation smack dab in the middle of your neighborhood? You give it a facelift with a funky decorative wall. The folks in the Hyde Park neighborhood needed a small park to enjoy during the days and evenings blessed by a moderate climate. Dogs, children, and seniors all flock to what is called Sparky Pocket Park, named for the 1930s substation's occasional emittance of a spark or two.

Cradled by crepe myrtles, elms, and holly, the former industrial site has a welcoming feel. However, Austinites have a penchant for putting a personal stamp on outdoor places. The concrete wall and old machinery around the substation did not mesh with the eclectic atmosphere of the area. Enter artist Berthold Haas who assessed the situation and created rock walls, arches, and mosaics made from karst stone, mirror balls, petrified wood, seashells, fossils, and broken pottery.

AN ELECTRIC EXPERIENCE

WHAT Sparky Park

WHERE 3701 Grooms St.

COST Free

PRO TIP When life gives you lemons, make lemonade. That is exactly what the community surrounding this park did when renovation of the substation left a tangle of wires and equipment. Take time to discover the found items that created a wonderful camouflage.

The art installation uses colorful materials to bring life to the rock walls that frame Sparky Park.

A jolt of creativity transformed the equipment and space around a former electric substation into an artful park.

The motif of electrical components comes across with colorful coils embedded in the three-dimensional art wall. Neighbors got into the act and contributed small toys to be incorporated into the wall. Some of the art installations even resemble miniature lighthouses. The public art became so popular that the city of Austin installed a bronze plaque at the site with the new name, "Grotto Wall at Sparky Park." It's a powerful neighborhood effort indeed.

COUNTRY MUSIC SPOKEN HERE

Do you hanker for the real honky-tonk experience?

James and Annetta White opened the Broken Spoke in 1964 to offer many new country-and-western acts the opportunity to gain an audience. George Strait and his Ace in the Hole band played the Spoke early in their careers. Legends such as Bob Wills, Roy Acuff, and Tex Ritter filled the hall. Willie Nelson was a regular and still visits. These days, you can expect to hear from Gary P. Nunn, the Derailers, and Dale Watson.

The atmosphere of the Spoke is a huge draw. Called "The Last of the True Texas Dancehalls," the decor gives truth to that claim. The interior is rustic with low ceilings, a concrete floor for dancing the two-step, and checkered cloths on tables lined up in the seating area surrounding the dance floor. At the far end is the raised bandstand. A museum/store fondly called the "Tourist Trap" displays mementos, photos, old signs, and souvenirs. In the past decade, the biggest change has been outside the hall. A $60 million mixed-use residential/retail project named the 704 invaded the Spoke's space. Two five-story buildings bookend the venue, showing the unfettered growth in the city of Austin. The good news is that the 704 provides new patrons, with 385 apartments.

In 2017, lucky patrons got a chance to hear legend Garth Brooks perform with his band. As far as folks dancing beside you, you just never know whom you might bump into. Photos on the wall show a grinning Clint Eastwood, a celebrity known

Enjoy an authentic dance hall experience and learn the two-step.

The Broken Spoke is tucked between modern new neighbors, but the music plays on.

SPOKEN FOR

WHAT Broken Spoke

WHERE 3201 S. Lamar Blvd.

COST Cover charge on Tuesdays $6. Dance lessons free. No cover charge for dinner and show evenings.

PRO TIP The Spoke is so famous that it has its own documentary, *Honky Tonk Heaven* (2016), which tells the story of the place that is "The last of the true Texas dance halls and damn sure proud of it."

to appreciate country-and-western music and dancing. Popular singing artist Harry Connick Jr. and Academy Award–winning director Quentin Tarantino have made the pilgrimage here as well.

If you're new to country/western dancing and want to master the Texas Two-Step, come at 7:30 p.m. to sign up for free lessons from 8 to 9 p.m. Wednesday through Saturday. Terri White, daughter of the owners, can get beginners comfortable with the steps. Food is served, ranging from barbecue to steaks, both country-fried and grilled.

EQUINE ROYALTY

What sculptor spent a year on a Texas ranch preparing to create a monumental Austin sculpture?

Alexander Phimister Proctor, renowned sculptor, had a true love of the West and its wide open spaces. Luckily for him, oilman Ralph Ogden and folklorist J. Frank Dobie gave him the chance of a lifetime, a commission to honor the mustang, the heroic steed of Texas.

To do right by the legendary horses, Proctor settled in at the Tom East Ranch in South Texas, home to one of the purest wild herds. He chose 15 candidates to observe and began the process. However, the mustangs weren't very cooperative subjects. Their strength and power made for some mighty unruly models, causing his ranch stay to extend to a full year.

Dobie, a lifelong admirer of the horse, wrote a book on mustang lore. He demanded perfection from Proctor. He had tremendous respect for this breed and its role in settling Texas. According to Dobie, "Spanish horse, Texas Cow Pony, and Mustang were all one in those times when, as sayings went, a man was no better than his horse, and a man on foot was no man at all." Fortunately, the sculptor shared his appreciation of the importance of these animals in *Seven Mustangs*, the sculpture he created.

However, not even the best-laid plans for finishing and installing the artwork could overcome an earth-shaking event that interceded—World War II. Launched in 1937 with its commission, the *Seven Mustangs* waited out the intervention of wartime to finally be completed and installed in May of 1948 on the University of Texas campus. This work, weighing nine tons, consists of seven mustangs sculpted in bronze—a stallion, five mares, and a colt. Proctor depicted the powerful horses in flight. They hardly seemed contained by the pedestal beneath them. This was Proctor's last commission and one of his most fulfilling.

The indomitable spirit and the wild beauty of mustangs race on in Alexander Phimister Proctor's magnificent sculpture.

HORSE POWER

WHAT *Seven Mustangs*

WHERE 2400 Trinity St., University of Texas campus

COST Free

PRO TIP If you stand directly in front of the statue, you will feel the power of the seven steeds careening down a hill.

Why did this work become so important in any study of the West? Horses gave the Native Americans and the pioneers their ability to survive on and cross the wild lands of North America. The Spanish explorers had brought the first horses to Mexico to aid in their conquest of the large region. Many of those original steeds roamed across the Rio Grande River, creating new herds used by indigenous peoples. The original steeds had the wonderful dual qualities of speed and endurance, carrying their riders long distances. Their strength and spirit served them well in the new land's frontier.

University of Texas students used to throw a net over the statue before taking on old Southwest Conference rivals, the Southern Methodist University Mustangs.

FIRST LADY

What was life really like for a young woman who lived here 11,000 years ago?

She liked ornaments and she liked to cook. Researchers could surmise such likelihoods from some of the artifacts found with the remains of a young woman who may have been among the earliest people ever to live in the Austin area. They named her Leanne, or the Leanderthal Lady, for the suburb northwest of Austin where she was found when road crews were doing work to connect Ranch Road 1431 to I-35. She was believed to have been from 18 to 25 years old when she died. Her careful burial included what must have been her most prized possessions—a fossilized shark's tooth that may have once been part of a necklace and a grinding stone. Her discovery was one of the oldest and most complete skeletons ever recovered in North America.

Research about Leanne and other Paleoindian discoveries continues at the Texas Archeological Research Laboratory at the University of Texas J. J. Pickle Research Campus, where her remains are preserved. The sprawling campus in North Austin, which isn't open to the public due to sensitive research,

LEANDERTHAL LADY

WHAT Texas Archeological Research Laboratory

WHERE University of Texas J. J. Pickle Research Campus, 10100 Burnet Rd.

COST Tours are $10 for adults.

PRO TIP Monthly tours at the Gault Archaeological Site north of Austin give visitors a close-up look at one of the most important Paleoindian sites in North America, where habitation dates back at least 14,000 years and digs have yielded more than 600,000 Clovis artifacts. For reservations, contact Clark Wernecke, executive director of the Gault School of Archaeological Research, at cwernecke@gaultschool.org or (512) 232-4912.

Left: A facial reconstruction by forensic specialists at Dow Corning shows what a prehistoric woman who lived in the Austin area 11,000 years ago looked like. Photo by Milton Bell, courtesy of Texas Beyond History, Texas Archaeological Research Laboratory at the University of Texas at Austin.

Right: Archeological research and many other fields of research are centered at the University of Texas J. J. Pickle Research Campus.

is home to dozens of research facilities in nuclear physics, chemistry, atmospheric science, and other fields. It was originally a magnesium plant that operated during World War II. After the war, two UT professors negotiated an agreement for the university to lease and eventually buy it. The site was expanded to 475 acres, but in 2003, the university agreed to a $130 million lease of some of its unused land for the development of high-end retail, office, and residential space at the neighboring Domain.

Leanne remains a lady of mystery and one of the first people to be drawn to the charm of the Austin area.

The research laboratory isn't open to the public, but it maintains the Texas Beyond History website (www.texasbeyondhistory.net) with excellent virtual exhibits and extensive educational information about its research activities.

IT'S A BIRD, IT'S A PLANE, IT'S A DINOSAUR

Where can you hang out with the world's largest flying animal?

The mammoth Texas Pterosaur that soars above the floor of the Texas Memorial Museum is the largest known flying animal that ever lived. It has a wingspan of 39 feet, about the size of a jet fighter, and it's a mighty big critter, even for Texas.

Douglas Lawson was a graduate student at the University of Texas when he first discovered the bone fragments of the creature in Big Bend National Park in 1971. He wasn't sure what they were, but when he and Texas Memorial Museum's Dr. Wann Langston Jr. examined them more closely, they realized the shape and hollow structure could only belong to a pterosaur. The find soon attracted worldwide attention. It was one of the most famous discoveries in the history of paleontology. Journals, newspapers, and radio and television broadcasts carried the story worldwide.

Lawson named the discovery *Quetzalcoatlus northropi*. The name combines the Aztec winged deity Quetzalcoati and aviation pioneer John Northrup, who built the flying wing, an airplane with a 230-foot wingspan. In case there was any doubt whether the Texas Pterosaur could get airborne, Caltech's Paul MacCready built a flying model of the winged monster in the mid-1980s.

Pterosaurs (pronounced "TARE-uh-soars") are thought to have lived about 65 million years ago. Researchers think it might have used its long legs to launch itself into the air. Most pterosaurs

---

HIGH FLYER

WHAT Texas Memorial Museum

WHERE 2400 Trinity St.

COST $7 adults, $5 children

PRO TIP The dinosaur-filled museum is an eye-opening educational experience for children.

Top: The pterosaur discovery is one of the biggest finds in the history of paleontology.

Inset: A prehistoric ancestor of the armadillo lived large.

lived near the sea and feasted on fish, but it's believed that the Texas Pterosaurs scavenged on dead dinosaurs or ate vulnerable babies. Researchers are still studying the specimens collected to develop new theories about the creatures. *Quetzalcoatlus northropi* attracted more notoriety when it was the featured specimen of National Fossil Day on October 17, 2018.

The giant replica flies high over dozens of other paleontological finds at the museum, but the museum holds an impressive herd of other ancient critters. There's a prehistoric ancestor of the armadillo nearly as big as a Volkswagen Beetle.

According to the Internet posts of a few true believers, some pterosaurs are still flying around. Three San Antonio elementary school teachers swore they saw one swoop low over them on a Texas highway in February 1976. An ambulance driver sighted one on a lonely road in Los Fresnos, Texas, in September 1982; and a private pilot in New York state reported a giant bird buzzed his airplane in May 1961.

STAR MAKER

Which Georgia Peach gifted the Lone Star Flag to the Yellow Rose state?

Texas in 1835 was struggling mightily to gain its freedom from Mexico and its identity as a land of opportunity. Texans, a ragtag, tired, and hungry band of likeminded settlers, were risking their lives fighting against a far greater force, Santa Anna and his army of thousands. The word spread throughout the Union, inspiring those who valued freedom above all else.

One of those was Joanna Troutman, an 18-year-old daughter of a well-to-do Georgia landowner. When a Georgia battalion saddled up to ride to the aid of the Texans, Troutman presented them with a banner she had made to represent the cause they were fighting for. Made of beautiful white silk and bearing a blue five-pointed star, the flag had two inscriptions— "Liberty or Death" on the front and, on the back, "Where Liberty dwells there is my country." Young Joanna, often called the "Betsy Ross" of Texas, showed great ingenuity in her flag's creation. Legend has it that the silk she used came from two of her own dresses. The banner owes its beauty to blue and white silk petticoats. It was carried to Texas, and Colonel James Fannin Jr., the commander at Fort Defiance, raised it over the fort at Goliad. What happened there cemented the flag's elevation to legendary status. The Texan fighting force was massacred, and the new flag was left in tatters but still waved. Thus began the iconic Lone Star.

Troutman never lived in Texas, but 34 years after her death in 1879, Texas governor Oscar B. Colquitt requested

Towering over 150 feet high, one of the tallest Texas flags in the state waves over the cemetery that is home to many famous Texans.

Joanna Troutman's flag flies high over her statue.

that she be moved to the Texas State Cemetery. Troutman is honored there with a bronze statue, as well as a portrait in the Capitol building. Both the statue and the painting capture the resolve of Ms. Troutman as she labors over the creation of what has come to be known as the Lone Star of Texas.

She watches over the capital city still.

WAVE THE FLAG

WHAT Joanna Troutman memorial monument

WHERE Texas State Cemetery, 909 Navasota St. Grounds open daily 8 a.m. to 5 p.m.

COST Free

PRO TIP A portrait of Joanna Troutman hangs in the Texas State Capitol, which has a fine representation of her holding the Lone Star Flag with the motto "Liberty or Death."

CLARA'S HEAVENLY LAGOON

Where is the most beautiful homesite in Austin?

Stephen F. Austin believed it was a lovely hillside on the bank of the Colorado River. He bought the land and planned to build his home there. Austin didn't live long enough to see his dream come true, but Clara Driscoll, known best as the "Savior of the Alamo," did. She and husband Hal Sevier, founder of the *Austin American* newspaper, built their dream house patterned after Italian villas they saw on their honeymoon at Lake Como. They named it Laguna Gloria, or "Heavenly Lagoon."

Clara left the house and its spacious grounds to the Texas Fine Arts Association in 1943, and it has been devoted to the arts ever since. The most recent addition is the Betty and Edward Marcus Sculpture Park, which showcases an exceptional collection of modern sculptures by Juan Muñoz, Tom Friedman, and more than 20 other artists.

GROUNDS FOR ART

WHAT The Contemporary Austin—Laguna Gloria

WHERE 3809 W. 35th St.

COST $10 adults, $5 seniors, under 18 free. Free to everyone on Tuesdays from 9 a.m. to 5 p.m.

PRO TIP Don't miss the museum shop for artistic gifts, children's games, toys, and handcrafted jewelry.

When the Alamo's Long Barracks was in danger of being razed to build a hotel, Clara Driscoll wrote the checks that saved it.

Top: Clara Driscoll's home on the lake is a center for art.

Inset: Tom Friedman's 33-foot stainless-steel figure titled Looking Up *welcomes visitors to the grounds.*

Whimsical *Lost Money,* by the Danish art group SUPERFLEX, attached 2,000 silver coins across the lakeside terrace, a nod to the financial crisis of 2008. But money can't match the serenity of a stroll across the 14-acre live oak–shaded grounds on a sunny afternoon. That's priceless.

FRIENDLY FLORA

How can you make giant flowers shine at night?

The name Mueller in Austin once meant a busy airport with nonstop overhead flights and noise pollution. The airport moved on to a new location, and Mueller now lends its name to a trend-setting, eco-friendly, energy-saving commercial and residential community.

What do you build to announce the arrival of a new-age neighborhood? In 2009, locals found out when 15 multifunctional pieces of architecture were installed adjacent to I-35. These structures became a well-planned field of monumental, manmade sunflowers. The humble sunflower, which in French is *tournesol* or "turns with the sun," is a perfect example of sustainability at work because it constantly turns its lovely head to catch the sun's rays.

These blue metal sunflowers stand 30 feet tall in the big Texas sky, artfully blocking the retail space and loading docks fronting IH-35. The use of the sunflower dovetails perfectly with the philosophy behind the Mueller development. Developers dedicated 140 acres of parkland planted with indigenous xeriscape in the residential /business area, ensuring availability of hike and bike trails, which are an Austin signature.

Mags Harries and Lajos Heder of Cambridge, Massachusetts, brought their considerable expertise to the project, having created more than 30 public art projects. *Sun Flowers—A Garden of Energy* is the name of this work that combines the beauty of architectural design with the idea of sustainability.

The Mueller neighborhood is home to a popular children's museum and one of the city's largest weekend farmers markets.

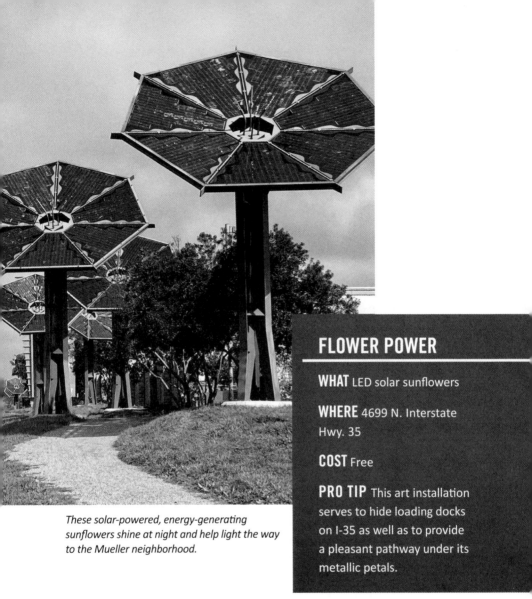

These solar-powered, energy-generating sunflowers shine at night and help light the way to the Mueller neighborhood.

FLOWER POWER

WHAT LED solar sunflowers

WHERE 4699 N. Interstate Hwy. 35

COST Free

PRO TIP This art installation serves to hide loading docks on I-35 as well as to provide a pleasant pathway under its metallic petals.

The Mueller community is a model of creative development, stressing mixed use building and energy efficiency. The beautiful flower structures with their geometric petal shapes use blue LED lighting to illuminate the community entrance at night. Each structure harnesses the sun's energy during the day, creating kilowatt hours of energy to light the structures, providing energy to the community, and returning power to the city.

TRAGEDY OF A TREE

Why did a jury send a man to prison for attempting to murder a tree?

A jilted suitor with a taste for the occult brought about one of the most talked about crimes in the city's history. It was an attack on a beloved resident of Austin. The injured party? A 600-year-old oak tree. Treaty Oak still stands in a quiet downtown neighborhood. It is a testament to a desire for peace in a land fraught with war and bloodshed. The famous oak is the reputed location of meetings between Stephen F. Austin and indigenous tribes, the Comanche and the Tonkawa. The tree is the last survivor of a grove of 14 stately oaks that were called the Council Oaks. It is cordoned off by a chain because the root system cannot stand the constant pounding of heavy tourist traffic. This majestic specimen was once in private hands, but the city purchased it for $1,000 in 1927.

Unfortunately, tragedy befell the towering specimen that had been placed in the National Forestry Hall of Fame. Austinite Paul Cullen poisoned the tree with the powerful herbicide Velpar. He spread the poison in a moon shape around the tree's roots, an act that gave rise to the rumor of occultism. The crime came to light in the spring of 1989 when visitors noticed the dying leaves and dead grass. The consensus of arborists was that Treaty Oak could not survive. Cullen was convicted of the crime and sentenced to nine years, although many Austinites called for him to receive the maximum penalty of life in prison. His reason for the crime? He was a victim of unrequited love and hoped to harness the

LUCKY IT WASN'T A HANGING TREE

WHAT Treaty Oak

WHERE Baylor Avenue between Fifth and Sixth Streets

COST Free

PRO TIP It's best to visit during daytime. Homeless folks sometimes frequent the area at night.

The mighty Treaty Oak was threatened by an assailant but survived.

spiritual energy of the ancient oak to turn the tide in his romantic life. Cullen served three years and was released. He died in El Centro, California, in 2001.

Experts went to work trimming the parts of the tree that were beyond hope of rehabilitation. Approximately two-thirds of it was lost. Treaty Oak captured the world's imagination, causing many people to pray for its reemergence against all odds. Miraculously, it did survive, producing acorns eight years later. One of these produced a tree that grows in front of city hall, and Austin became a city known for its environmental conscience, passing one of the first tree protection ordinances in America.

It's a tree that keeps giving.

When it was fighting for its life, well-wishers sometimes left chicken soup at the base of the tree. It couldn't hurt!

123

STROLLIN' DOWN THE RIVER

What makes a river so poetic? "A good river is nature's life work in song."–Mark Helprin

There aren't too many rivers in Texas you can walk across without getting your feet wet. But you'll find one in the 2nd Street District. Spanning 40 feet of sidewalk, the artwork beneath your feet represents the flow of the Brazos River from its headwaters to the Gulf of Mexico. Artist Ryah Christensen created the mosaic through careful placement of broken tile and rock to reveal the change in course of the Brazos as it winds its way through Texas to its ultimate destination. Symbolic representations of the wildlife that populates the region abound. Christensen also depicts the people who relied on the Brazos for their very existence and for their ability to traverse geographical regions. They weren't the only ones who needed the waters to survive—their livestock and crops did too. Swirls and eddies are illustrated with vibrant colors of dark blue, turquoise, obsidian, emerald, and crimson.

The Brazos River, which the Spanish knew as "the river of the arms of God," played a huge role in Texas history. Stretching across the state for 840 miles, it provided sustenance and a lifeline for pioneers. With the advent of dams and electricity, Texas rivers helped light up communities large and small.

This installation is a part of future artwork planned for the intersections of numbered streets with those named for rivers.

A mural in the sidewalk traces the course of the Brazos River through the state.

ECOND STREET

A RIVER RUNS THROUGH IT

WHAT Brazos River mosaic

WHERE Second Avenue and Brazos Street

COST Parking

PRO TIP This metaphorical representation of the Brazos River is but a part of the city's Public Art Plan that highlights Austin's dependence on its greatest resource—water.

The Brazos mural is also a reminder of how rivers play prominently in the street layout of Austin. North/south downtown streets such as Brazos and Guadalupe are named for Texas rivers and are placed in the same order as they are on the map. They all "flow" into Lady Bird Lake.

A BLONDE ICON

Who can turn the world on with her smile?

Adjacent to an Austin hair salon, a beautiful blonde with blinding perfect white teeth smiles at motorists and pedestrians. Her flowing blonde mane is always picture perfect.

Stefanie Distefano, an Austin multimedia artist, created a larger than life mosaic of iconic Texan Farrah Fawcett. The artwork, made of glass and ceramic, fills a wall that faces the street and greets customers. Having Fawcett's beautiful mane grace an art wall in front of a beauty salon is an obvious choice. However, the actress's contributions to the Austin art world are well known. Studying with the famous sculptor Charles Umlauf while a student at the University of Texas, Ms. Fawcett found her true passion—sculpture. Many of her works have been featured at the Umlauf Sculpture Garden and Museum.

Holding a daisy, Fawcett is surrounded by three angels appropriately brandishing a variety of hairbrushes. The vibrant blue background created of varying shades of broken tiles is punctuated by small roses. Fawcett, an artist herself, would've appreciated the community collaboration of bringing the installation to life. Distefano credits as many as 100 community members with helping piece together the many broken mirrors and tiles.

AUSTIN'S ANGEL

WHAT Farrah Fawcett mosaic mural

WHERE 500 W. Oltorf St. outside Salon Sovay

COST Free

PRO TIP Salon Sovay's sister salon at 2444 S. First St. has its own Fawcett tribute, a painted mural, complete with ethereal clouds and floating angels wielding round brushes.

A mosaic at one of the city's most popular hair salons commemorates the former Austin art student who went on to fame in Hollywood.

"There'll end up being 100 people working on a piece and it's such a magical experience," Distefano said. "My work is free-spirited and so openhearted that everybody finds their voice in it, which tells you something about Austin."

A mosaic outside a popular Austin hair salon pays tribute to the former University of Texas student who became a movie starlet and introduced the world to big hair.

THE CHITLIN' CIRCUIT

Can you hear the blues in the Austin night?

Old East Austin nurtured the soul of the city. And that soul carried with it a melody. It was the sound of the blues mixed with gospel. To find it, folks strolled down to the Victory Grill to hear Bobby "Blue" Bland's rhythm and blues rendition of "That's the Way Love Is."

The Victory Grill, opened by band manager Johnny Holmes on August 17, 1945, started as a gathering spot for African American soldiers returning from war to the segregated South. Holmes named his club for the victory won by the allies in 1945. The Grill was a hot spot on the "Chitlin Circuit," places that were friendly to African Americans, spotlighting artists and music that did not receive wide acceptance. The term "Chitlin" referred to chitterlings, or pig intestines, a part of the hog that was less desirable. However, African American cooks worked wonders with cheap cuts. Chitlins symbolize the ability of the Black community to make something tasty out of that which is often discarded.

The Grill had humble beginnings but moved to a larger place to accommodate a large clientele. Black performers flocked to the Grill. Godfather of Soul James Brown rocked the building with his energetic shows full of percussion and those iconic dance moves. Billie Holiday and Etta James entertained with their soulful renditions. Ike and Tina Turner came with their band and the gritty vocals of their lead singer. The Bobby "Blue" Bland Band drew the crowds.

WINNING MUSIC

WHAT Victory Grill

WHERE 1104 E. 11th St.

COST Free to see the historic site

PRO TIP Check out the vibrant murals on the side of the Victory Grill Building memorializing the intertwined history of soul food and blues music in the capital city.

Tina Turner, James Brown, and other stars played the Victory Grill in the days of segregation.

Victory Grill remained popular until a sea change occurred in Austin. Segregation ended. Many of the club's patrons could move elsewhere and did so. White acts such as Janis Joplin still played at the Grill, bringing large crowds of white and Black Austinites together, united by a love of blues.

This club had a roller-coaster ride from the 1970s until its closing due to loss of revenue on the music side of the business. The restaurant itself stayed a draw with its Southern menu, but a fire in the 1980s and lackluster profitability over the decades led to its closing in 2017. However, the Victory Grill was added to the National Register of Historic Places in 1998 in honor of its cultural importance, and the building still stands, ready for its encore.

Murals on the building's exterior tell a tale of music and civil rights.

SERVANT GIRL ANNIHILATOR

Was Austin's version of "Jack the Ripper" ever found?

Austin endured a series of horrific murders beginning in 1884 by a killer whose methods resembled the gruesome handiwork that was later a trademark of Jack the Ripper in Whitechapel. William Sidney Porter, better known as O. Henry, was a resident and prolific short story author who actually named this grisly murderer. In a letter to his friend Dave Hall dated May 1885, O. Henry wrote, "Town is fearfully dull, except for the frequent raids of the Servant Girl Annihilators, who make things lively during the dead hours of the night; if it were not for them, items of interest would be very scarce, as you may see by the *Statesman*."

During this time period, servants often lived in the homes of their employers. These crimes were clustered in a downtown area bordered by the Driskill Hotel, Scholz Garten, and what is now a popular music venue, the Scoot Inn. Young girls were abducted in their sleep from their bedrooms in their employers' homes at midnight. Outside the homes, the perpetrator wielded an ax with a vengeance as he mutilated his poor victims, striking again and again without mercy. Acting in a rage, he nonetheless tried to avoid detection by discarding his boots before entering the homes. However, his bloody footprints gave him away as he lacked a fifth toe on one foot. That information was kept secret by

ONE REMEMBERED

WHAT Grave of Last Known Victim

WHERE Oakwood Cemetery 1601 Navasota St.

COST Free

PRO TIP This murderer, nicknamed the Annihilator by O. Henry, blazed a bloody trail across Austin, killing defenseless women. For an updated analysis, look for the PBS series *History Detectives* and the episode on the case.

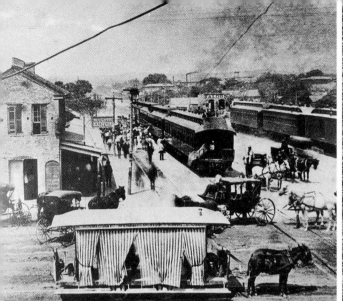

Left: A grisly serial killer whose methods resembled Jack the Ripper spread terror through Austin in the late 1800s.

Right: A tombstone in Oakwood Cemetery marks the resting place of the Austin mass murderer's last victim.

police. These murders continued from 1884 until Christmas of 1885, taking eight lives of young girls who might have faded into history, except for O. Henry's letter and the notoriety of Jack the Ripper's subsequent London mayhem. Some even speculated that the two might be the same killer.

Who was the perpetrator? In February 1886, Nathan Elgin abducted a woman from a saloon and began mercilessly beating her, bringing the attention of citizens and police. The saloon was across the street from what is now the Scoot Inn. In the fight with Elgin, police officer John Bracken shot the enraged man. During an autopsy, his missing toe became evident. Crime solved. Perhaps.

The victims were buried in the Austin Cemetery now known as Oakwood Cemetery. Due to their station in life, the women did not have gravestones; however, one of the last victims, Susan Hancock, was a middle-class woman who did have a marker. It reads: "Mother. Tho' lost to sight to memory dear."

Austin's first mass murderer cut a wide swath across Austin's neighborhoods.

THE SPIRITS OF THE DRISKILL

At which hotel do ghosts and politicians make strange bedfellows?

The Driskill Hotel was built in 1886 by Colonel Jesse Driskill, a native Tennessean who made his fortune in in his adopted home of Texas by selling cattle to the Confederacy. The cost of the project was $400,000, and it became known as one of the nation's finest hotels. Upon entering the brick-and-limestone hotel, you'll see beautiful Texas touches throughout the grand first floor. Original columns still grace the hallway and flank the arches. Handmade architectural details and original hand paintings have been preserved in many of the rooms.

The financial history of the graceful landmark has the tempo of a thrill ride. The elegant hotel has escaped bankruptcies, economic downturns, droughts, threats of demolition, and

LOST IN A POKER GAME

WHAT The historic Driskill Hotel

WHERE 604 Brazos St.

COST Rooms start at $179 per night; call (512) 439-1234.

PRO TIP Visit the Maximillian Room and view the beautiful mirrors created to honor the Empress Carlotta and bearing her image in their frames. Don't miss the photographs and news stories outside the LBJ Suite and the Jim Hogg Parlor.

The purchase of a corner lot in downtown Austin for $7,500 in the 1880s proved to be a very savvy business move for Colonel Jesse Driskill. The hotel he erected on this site has remained one of the most popular and iconic in the state.

Visitors who want to experience the beauty and feel of the Driskill can see many historic architectural features, portraits, and exhibits on view in the lobby and public areas.

rumors of haunted portraits and suites. In fact, you can add the legend that Jesse Driskill lost the hotel in a poker game. The jury is out on that one.

The history of the Driskill is populated by many famous Texas politicians. Miriam "Ma" Ferguson, the first woman governor of Texas, danced at her inaugural ball in the elegant halls of the hotel, as did Ann Richards decades later after her gubernatorial win. Another famous figure is tied to the hotel both personally and politically. President Lyndon B. Johnson had his first date with future wife Claudia "Lady Bird" Taylor in the dining room. The future couple had been introduced the previous day at the Capitol. In 1948, LBJ waited for Senate election results while enjoying the comfort of the hotel's Jim Hogg Parlor. The hotel proved to be good luck for his political career as he and his family also awaited his presidential win with positive election results in 1964.

The Driskill has been home not only to famous cattle barons and politicians, but also to the folk lore of larger-than-life criminals. In 1934, the Texas Rangers took over the Jim Hogg Parlor to make plans to capture the most wanted couple of the day, Bonnie Parker and Clyde Barrow.

For fans of the supernatural, the Driskill offers a haunted history. Two rooms, 429 and 525, have become a part of Austin's haunted lore. According to legend, two new brides on their honeymoon took their lives years apart in the bathrooms of those suites. Visitors who have since occupied those rooms have reported hearing voices and having clothing mysteriously packed for them. That's hotel service not requiring a tip.

DISCOVERING THE DINOS

The tracks these ancient critters left are huge. Can you hear them roar?

Northwest of Austin where US 183 north crosses the North San Gabriel River, amateur paleontologists can satisfy their hankering to experience ancient Hill Country inhabitants up close and personal.

It isn't a park, but access to the riverbed is open to the public. The large, distinctive tracks have been an attraction for decades, but their existence has mainly been passed along by word of mouth.

On pleasant, sunny weekends, visitors park on the south side of the US 183 bridge and hike for a mile west along the riverbed. At the river's edge, they encounter a line of distinctive footprints that mark the path of prehistoric creatures that passed this way in the marshes of the Cretaceous period thought to be 65 million years ago. It was perfect ground for leaving prints that would be baked by the hot temperatures of later periods. Eventually they were covered, only to be revealed again in modern times.

YOUR OWN JURASSIC PARK

WHAT Dinosaur tracks

WHERE Park on the south side of the US 183 bridge at 601 S. Gabriel Dr. in Leander.

COST Free

PRO TIP The tracks are only visible in dry weather when the riverbed is exposed. Usually dry summer months are best. It's a walk of approximately one mile from the bridge to the tracks. Wear appropriate footwear. There aren't any restrooms or direction signs.

For an off-the-beaten path adventure, follow the giant tracks dinosaurs left in the bed of the North San Gabriel River.

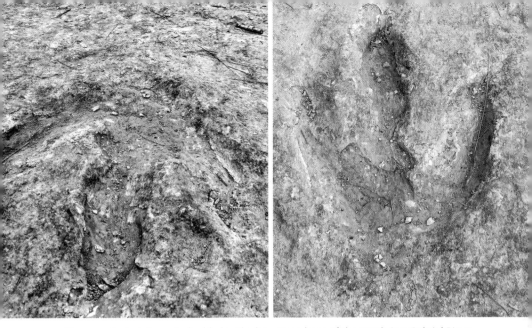

Dinosaur footprints are imbedded in the limestone base of the North San Gabriel River. (Photographs by Philip Thomas.)

There are more than a dozen examples of theropod tracks, made by three-toed dinosaurs that follow a trail of other prints made by creatures with round foot pads. The prints with three strong toes and claws are carnivores. The dinosaurs with pronounced round foot pads are herbivores. From the proximity of the tracks, it's easy to imagine that a chase between hunter and hunted took place here long ago. Running is a hugely popular exercise in Austin, and apparently it was practiced in prehistoric times too. But it appears that some of the earliest inhabitants were running for their lives.

CERVEZA AND LEGENDS

Why does the historic Scoot Inn, a local watering hole and music venue, keep giving up remnants of old Austin?

Just imagine a hot August Austin day in 1871 when the sun beats down mercilessly and the dusty streets are populated by tired dogs and wagons rolling into town. Travelers came to Austin either to settle or as a way station to somewhere else. The first things you might want after a grueling trip would be a cool drink and a few groceries to revive your spirits and carry you on your way. Scoot Inn could fill the bill.

Located next to the railroad line in East Austin, it began as a grocery store. The rustic wooden structure had dirt floors and a humble interior. The floors were eventually finished, but much of the rest of the building didn't change much. Over the course of its history, remnants of the long-ago railroad line still appear occasionally on the property— railroad spikes, bits of iron, and other relics.

In the 1880s, the Inn became a saloon. It cemented its place in local lore when it became the scene of a crime by the infamous Austin ax murderer known as the Servant Girl Annihilator. The episode at the Scoot Inn led to the apprehension of the suspected killer.

In its current iteration, the Scoot is a music venue with both live bands and DJs, as well as a beer garden for hot nights and an outdoor concert venue. Indie bands are a favorite at this East Austin establishment. Be ready to brave the Texas heat since much of the entertainment is outside. If you're

SONGS AND SUDS

WHAT Scoot Inn

WHERE 1308 E. Fourth St.

COST On music nights, cover charge for two is about $35.

PRO TIP Come early to get cheaper parking.

The Scoot Inn is one of the city's oldest saloons.

feeling the temperature climb, step inside the air-conditioned bar for a brew, a cocktail, or a chilled rosé. Except for air conditioning, the creature comforts haven't changed much here since 1871.

The Scoot Inn is hidden away in East Austin but is a popular music venue. It was also a part of a grisly crime by the ax murderer known as the Servant Girl Annihilator.

DON'T COME AND TAKE IT

Without Angelina Eberly would Austin be just another Waco with better scenery?

They call it the Archive War. It was short-lived, but it might have had disastrous consequences for Austin if it hadn't been for an alert, spunky innkeeper. On an early morning in 1842, Angelina Eberly noticed unusual activity around the General Land Office near her inn. Alarmed, she fired a cannon kept around for defense against intruders. It alerted the citizenry that interlopers sent by Sam Houston were attempting to take the state archives. Houston wanted them removed to Washington on the Brazos for safe keeping.

Austinites, who saw it as a blatant attempt to steal away the capital, gave chase and retrieved the archives near Round Rock, without a fight.

Angelina, who was honored in recent years with a statue on Congress Avenue that depicts her beside her trusty cannon, was a long-forgotten heroine. She moved to Texas in the 1820s and, with her first husband, opened an inn at San Felipe de Austin. Unfortunately, hostilities

LOCKED AND LOADED

WHAT Angelina Eberly statue

WHERE Congress Avenue and Sixth Street

COST Parking

PRO TIP Walk down Congress Avenue toward the Capitol Building. You'll put yourself squarely in the crosshairs of Mrs. Eberly as she stands ready to unload six pounds of grapeshot pellets at those bent on making off with the state archives.

Quick-thinking innkeeper Angelina Eberly is one of the unsung heroines of Austin. Her cannon shot was a wake-up call that helped keep the capital from moving away.

A bronze statue created by Pat Oliphant in honor of this strong Texas woman stands at the location of her fierce cannon volley on behalf of her city.

with Mexico caused the destruction of the town and the loss of their business. Subsequently widowed, she moved to Bastrop and married Captain Jacob Eberly. A business opportunity took them to Austin and the opening of the Eberly House, a popular tavern and lodging place frequented by Mirabeau B. Lamar, Sam Houston, and many other prominent people.

Angelina became an ardent supporter of her new community and a popular hostess. But her most important service as an innkeeper was sounding the wake-up call that saved the city.

SWAY TO THE SMOKY SWEET BLUES

How did Antone's change the music scene?

Antone's is the result of a love affair between one man and the blues. Clifford Antone came to Austin from Port Arthur in the late '60s for college, but an early brush with the law ended that. However, he came away with a true appreciation for the blues, music that had been nurtured in East Austin by the clubs in the African American community. In 1975, in what had been a furniture store, Antone opened his eponymous club on Sixth Street, a downtown Austin area that had fallen on hard times. Even landmarks such as the famous Driskill Hotel were suffering a fallow period. He took quite a gamble with that investment in a city that had fallen hard for psychedelic rock in the past decade and that now was leaning heavily toward Southern rock music.

However, the early musicians that came to his gritty venue opened the door artistically for blues musicians of all stripes to gain a foothold in a city that was just becoming a music center. He invited zydeco artist Clifton Chenier and his Red Hot Louisiana Band for a weekend performance that cemented the lane that the club owner had

MUSIC MAKERS

WHAT Antone's Nightclub (www.antonesnightclub.com)

WHERE 305 E. Fifth St

COST All shows are general admission. Purchase tickets in advance online.

PRO TIP Check out YouTube (youtube.com) for clips from the award-winning documentary *Antone's, Home of the Blues* (2004), a behind-the-scenes look at the magic that is this iconic venue.

Visit this club and find out why it's called "Home of the Blues."

Antone's has been a home for blues in Austin since 1975.

created in a city that would become known as the Live Music Capital, in no small part due to this entrepreneur. Other acts followed. The Fabulous Thunderbirds brought their Texas blues style, marked by electric guitars, keyboards, and harmonica. Stevie Ray Vaughan, a future Austin icon, brought his blues sounds from Dallas with his Triple Threat Review. His hard driving guitar licks became legendary. The crowds came to hear the artists from across the country who were drawn to Austin by Clifford Antone's ability to provide them a welcoming and rocking venue.

Antone's was a peripatetic enterprise, moving to a series of locations in Austin but still putting on first rate shows with famous performers such as B. B. King, Buddy Guy, Bobby Blue Bland, Ray Charles, Stevie Ray Vaughan and Double Trouble, and Gary Clark Jr. The club's house band drew praise, with W. C. Clark becoming an Austin favorite. It was also quite a draw for celebrities and music royalty. You might brush shoulders with music fan Clint Eastwood or see U2 or Bob Dylan listening to a set.

The Austin music scene underwent a change when old venues such as the Armadillo World Headquarters and Victory Grill closed. Other clubs opened in their place, giving artists alternate venues. Clifford died in 2006, leaving the business in his sister's hands. It settled into a quieter phase before closing. However, blues had gained a foothold in Austin, and Antone's still had its army of fans. Opening again on Fifth Street in the past decade, the Antone family came full circle, bringing the authentic blues back to downtown.

A BALANCING ACT

How many boats can you stack on a pedestal?

When you stroll down the brick-lined Speedway pedestrian walkway, don't be surprised by a traffic jam looming overhead. Only this jam is intentional. *Monochrome for Austin* is a 50-foot-tall metal sculpture made of 75 interwoven aluminum canoes and an occasional fishing boat raised high on a pedestal outside the Hackerman Building. Recycling is near and dear to the hearts of Austinites. The sculpture certainly plays into the idea of reuse and recycle. Many of these boats were damaged vessels donated by local boat rental companies. Another consideration in Austin is the capricious attitude of Mother Nature. Strong winds funneling down a walkway can do much damage to outdoor art, especially one with so many heavy interlocking parts that are posed to seemingly defy gravity. Looking up at the sculpture, visitors will see strong cables enveloping and anchoring the artwork. It is both an architectural and engineering feat.

Monochrome is a part of the Landmarks project, an ongoing privately funded effort that will install art along the pedestrian walkway between Martin Luther King Jr. Boulevard and Dean Keeton Street. Artist Nancy Rubins is the first female sculptor chosen for such a project by Landmarks. Andrée Bober, the project's director, said that all future installations will be chosen for their ability to communicate with those who use the walkway. The art is close, accessible to all, and free of charge. Just don't ask the artist what the work means. She's leaving it up to you, the audience.

The Landmarks project sculpture brings character to the pedestrian walkway, giving passersby a chance to enjoy a boat balancing act.

This huge sculpture hangs above the street like a canoe collision in midair.

DON'T ROCK THE BOAT

WHAT *Monochrome for Austin*

WHERE The Hackerman Building on Speedway and 24th Street

COST Free

PRO TIP To see the accelerated version of the building of this kayak sculpture, go to austin.culturemap.com and search for "Watch the largest sculpture in University of Texas history come to life."

143

THE PIG WAR

How did a few pigs cost France an empire?

In 1804, Napoleon gave away lands that doubled the size of the United States in the Louisiana Purchase. But France might have laid claim to a new empire in Texas, except for the swine intervention of a few pigs. The pigs were the last straw for Jean Pierre Isidore Alphonse Dubois de Saligny. The French chargé d'affaires was busy building his headquarters, the French Legation, one of the grandest structures in the fledgling city when it was the capital of the Republic of Texas. But Austin was too rough for his taste. Trespassing pigs, owned by innkeeper Richard Bullock, trashed the home of the French diplomat, gorging on his fine linens and diplomatic papers. Saligny sent his butler to shoot the pigs. Bullock thrashed the butler and threatened to thrash Saligny.

The aloof delegate was already in hot water for spending counterfeit money and passing himself off as a count. He retreated back to New Orleans in a snit. The Franco-Texian Bill, which Saligny advocated, proposed to bring 8,000 French families to Texas. They were to be protected by 8,000 French soldiers and 20 forts on three million acres ceded by the Texas government. The bill failed, but the French Legation survived as Austin's oldest frame home. The Greek Revival and raised cottage-style landmark was Austin's grandest structure when it was finished in 1841.

Money was scarce when Austin was the rough-hewn capital of the Republic of Texas, so France's proposal to fund a vast settlement was tempting to many.

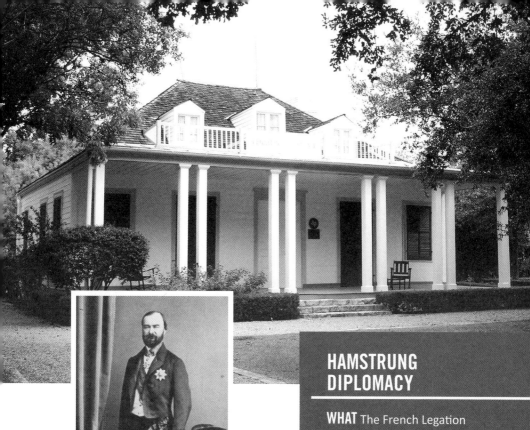

Top: The Texas Historical Commission took over operation of the museum in 2017 and began an extensive renovation of the city's oldest frame building. Photos courtesy of the French Legation State Historic Site, Historic Sites Division; THC Texas Historical Commission, 2017.

Inset: Austin was too rough-hewn for France's emissary to the Republic of Texas.

HAMSTRUNG DIPLOMACY

WHAT The French Legation Museum State Historic Site

WHERE 802 San Marcos St.

COST To be set after the restoration is completed in late 2020; (512) 463-7948.

PRO TIP If you hear shouts and yells in French on the 2 ½-acre grounds, it's probably members of the Heart of Texas Pentanque Club. They often come to the French Legation to play pentanque, a French lawn game. It's similar to pitching pennies but played with a 2-pound ball and a lot of enthusiasm.

AGGIES STORMED THE CASTLE

Did the Aggies take the "West Point of the South" away from Austin?

It sits on the crown of a hill overlooking downtown and Shoal Creek, but the "Castle" is almost forgotten. It held big dreams once. In 1870, the formidable turret-topped structure rose as one of the main buildings of the Texas Military Institute. City leaders raised $10,000 in gold to persuade the military school to move from Bastrop. Spread across 32 acres on Castle Hill, its buildings were patterned after the Virginia Military Institute and West Point. Supporters hoped it might become the West Point of the South.

Texas A&M had other ideas. Founded in 1876, the school was floundering under its first president. It needed new leadership. Col. John Garland James, the respected president of Texas Military Institute, was hired. Most of the faculty joined him. Without its select cadre of educators, Texas Military Institute closed in 1878.

The main building preserves one of the four turret towers that were originally planned for each of the four corners of the school's square. A barrack provided housing for 400 students. After the Civil War, when military instruction was frowned on, most of the classes focused on literary studies and science. Any military training was for exercise purposes only. Tuition, including room and board, was $375 a year. Now renovated

A castle that was once one of the city's proudest landmarks still holds its ground on a lofty hill downtown.

The building known as the Castle was once the crown jewel of the Texas Military Institute.

and used as offices, it is one of the oldest college buildings in Texas. One of its previous owners was controversial developer Gary Bradley who fought determined battles with the city's environmental activists for years.

ALMOST ANOTHER WEST POINT

WHAT The Castle

WHERE 1111 W. 11th St.

PRO TIP Visitors can see the Castle and its grounds from 11th Street that dead ends at a bluff, but the Castle itself is not open to the public. It is used as offices for Castle Hill Partners.

THINK OR SWIM

Why was a rock at the city's favorite swimming pool reserved for great thinkers?

At the edge of Barton Springs, a monumental bronze statue honors three of Austin's most beloved literary figures.

They seem so animated in Glenna Goodacre's fine sculpture, you could almost believe the three friends had just gathered the way they always did on a sunny afternoon to engage each other in lively conversation. J. Frank Dobie, the father of Texas folklore, is reaching his hand out toward a book that naturalist Roy Bedichek is holding. Walter Prescott Webb, the preeminent Southwestern historian of his era, has his pants legs rolled up, wading in the cold spring water like he often did. He wasn't a swimmer. Bedichek, on the other hand, immersed himself in nature's refreshing touch. They say he would stand up, lean backwards, and fall into the water just above Parthenia Spring, the largest of the fountains that fills Austin's favorite swimming hole. Bedichek drove there every afternoon at 3:30 from July through October for 40 years until his death in 1959.

A flood in the 1960s washed away the rock that was once their sunny literary salon. But its memory lives on at *Philosopher's Rock*, funded by Capital Area Statues Inc. and installed in 1994 as one of the group's first sculptures of iconic Austin figures. Children, on their way to a swim, often climb around the feet of the three grandfatherly figures. Others stop to read some of their thoughts inscribed on plaques around the

SWIM TEAM

WHAT *Philosopher's Rock*

WHERE Near the bathhouse and entrance to Barton Springs Pool

COST Free

PRO TIP Jump in and see for yourself why Barton Springs Pool is so beloved. It's open year-round, and the spring-fed water stays at a constant 68 degrees.

Three Texas giants gather around Barton Springs for conversation and friendship.

base. Steve Moore, a former playwrighting fellow at the Michener Center for Writers, said the statues inspired him to write *Nightswim*, a 2004 play about Dobie, Webb, and Bedichek. The three had similar small-town roots and grew up at a time when the memory of the frontier was still fresh. But they had an openness to thought. Moore believes they helped change the course of the city. "Under their influence," he wrote, "Austin made a shift from typical Texas town to an oasis of open-mindedness."

The homes of J. Frank Dobie (now a writer's center) and Walter Prescott Webb are preserved, but the house near campus where Bedichek lived and studied the city's flora and fauna was razed to become part of the parking lot at the LBJ Library. Glenna Goodacre, sculptor of *Philosopher's Rock*, also sculpted the *Vietnam Women's Memorial* in Washington, DC, and the likeness of Sacajawea on the $1 coin.

HOME OF THE HILLTOPPERS

Where is the best view of downtown Austin?

Take a look from the hilltop campus of St. Ed's. It's one of the best places to enjoy a panoramic overlook.

HIGHER EDUCATION AT ST. ED'S

WHAT St. Edward's University Main Hall

WHERE 3001 S. Congress Ave.

PRO TIP Unlike most other universities, St. Ed's has an open campus, making it easy to tour by car.

When the Rev. Edward Sorin came to Austin in 1872 to scout the location for a new Catholic school, he had already founded a small school in South Bend, Indiana, that turned out pretty well. It became the University of Notre Dame. The Austin school was St. Edwards Academy, named for his patron saint, Edward the Confessor and King. It turned out pretty well too.

St. Ed's, as the students like to call it, crowns a hill in South Austin that offers what arguably is the best view of Austin's skyline. A centerpiece of the campus is one of Austin's most beautiful landmark buildings, the limestone-clad, four-story Main Building. Famed Galveston architect Nicholas Clayton designed it in 1888. He also oversaw its rebuilding in 1903 when it was heavily damaged by fire. It was a big step up from the school's humble beginnings in 1878. Three farm boys made up the first student body. They met in a converted building on the South Austin farm that Mary Doyle left to the Catholic Church. When the Rev. Sorin visited, he was impressed with the beauty of the hills and lakes. Sorin Oak, one of the city's largest live oaks, spreads its shady branches near Main Hall. It is named for him.

Top: Famed Galveston architect Nicholas Clayton designed the Main Building.

Inset: St. Ed's hilltop campus overlooks the city's skyline.

St. Ed's had an undergraduate enrollment of 4,301 students in 2018. Its sports teams, which compete in NCAA Division II, are called, appropriately enough, the Hilltoppers.

The Rev. Edward Sorin, founder of St. Edward's University, also founded the University of Notre Dame, where he spent most of his life.

THE PARAMOUNT STILL SHINES

How did one of the city's biggest neon signs, almost five stories tall, vanish without a trace?

Magic still happens on the stage of Austin's oldest theater, now beautifully restored. But preservationists are haunted by the mystery of its giant neon sign, called a "blade," that mysteriously vanished. It was taken down for renovation in 1963, never to be seen again. It wasn't a small thing to lose. In 1930, the *Austin-American Statesman* described it as a "huge sign, more than 75 feet high (from the sidewalk) and topped with a brilliant sunburst."

The theater opened as a vaudeville house in 1915. The sign went up after Paramount Pictures purchased it in 1930. For decades, it lighted the way to the landmark theater on Congress Avenue. After the theater was saved from demolition in 1973, restoration began on its ornate interior, but no amount of searching would reveal the sign. The namesake light finally made its encore when the theater celebrated its 100th anniversary in 2015. Cranes hoisted a 47-foot reproduction of the original to the front of the Register of National Historic Places landmark. Built at a cost of almost $200,000, it shines brightly over the 250-plus performances and events the Paramount hosts each year.

ON WITH THE SHOW

WHAT Paramount Theatre

WHERE 713 Congress Ave.

COST Ticket prices vary. Contact the box office at www.theatreaustin.org or (512) 472-5470.

PRO TIP The Moontower Comedy Festival, founded in 2012, is one of the theater's most popular new events. It features well-known touring performers and rising stars.

Magic still happens on the stage of Austin's oldest theater.

The theater continues to be a favorite venue for concerts, stage shows, and movies. It has hosted many world movie premiers, from recent screenings at the South by Southwest festival to *the Best Little Whorehouse in Texas*, which featured a parade down Congress Avenue led by Dolly Parton and Burt Reynolds in 1982.

When no color photographs could be found of the Paramount's missing "blade," restorers used postcards to pick the colors for the new one, which is green with a yellow border and red sunburst on top.

CONVICT HILL LEFT ITS MARK

Do the ghosts of men in chains who worked there still haunt Convict Hill?

The scars of the limestone they chiseled still remain, but not much else. Gone is the clinking of their chains. So is the hardship and the hunger they endured and the misery they felt as they toiled in the hot Texas sun, working from daybreak till dark. Quarrying limestone for the Texas Capitol, they heaved out tons of it—so much that a six-mile-long railroad was built to deliver it to downtown Austin from Convict Hill.

To save money on construction, the state hired out prison laborers to contactors and paid them nothing. "Living on the hill was not much better than dying," *Austin American-Statesman* reporter Betty McNabb wrote in 1972. A roster listed the ages of laborers. One was 10. His name was L. S. Beauregard. A note on the ledger read, "Bad boy, several times punished."

Legend says at least eight men died. Their bodies were never found, but a developer tried in 1985. He hired an archeologist to look for traces, but nothing was found. He hired investigators to comb historical records, prison reports, and any other shred of evidence they could find. Still nothing.

STONE COLD GHOSTS

WHAT Convict Hill

WHERE Convict Hill Quarry Park, 6511 Convict Hill Rd.

COST Free

PRO TIP The park offers a short hiking trail, but there are no restrooms or other facilities.

Prisoners labored—and possibly died—to dig the stone for the state capitol at Convict Hill.

Top: Trails lead through the quarry at Convict Hill.

Inset: Convict labor furnished limestone for the capitol.

The limestone was used for foundations and part of the inner structure of the capitol, but by 1886 builders realized that it couldn't be used on the exterior because it contained minerals that discolored it when exposed to weather. Plans were made to use granite from Marble Falls instead. Another rail line was built to haul it to Austin. By 1888, the rails to Convict Hill were no longer needed, and they were removed. The prisoners were gone too, but Convict Hill was left to whisper its secrets to anyone who would listen.

THE DAY THE DILLO DIED

How did the iconic Armadillo World Headquarters end up as roadkill?

Cofounder Eddie Wilson picked the name in part because the building was once a National Guard armory. Built like tiny armored tanks, armadillos were ubiquitous around Austin. So the Armadillo World Headquarters was born with its first shows in the summer of 1970.

The late Gov. Ann Richards recalled that just before it opened, Wilson showed her "the great big old building that looked like it was about to be demolished" and told her it "would become the center of the music universe." Oddly enough, it just about did. Often called just the "Dillo," the music hall lured national touring acts and ushered in the era of "cosmic" cowboys. Willie Nelson played there often. So did scores of others, from Bruce Springsteen to ZZ Top (without the beards).

Despite its success and national notoriety, the Dillo was always on slippery financial footing. Bankruptcy was filed in 1977, and the city's burgeoning growth amped up the value of the 5.62 acres it sat on. The landlord is said to have sold it for between $4 million and $8

THE LATE GREAT ARMADILLO

WHAT Site of the former Armadillo World Headquarters

WHERE 505 Barton Springs Rd.

COST Free

PRO TIP It takes some looking to find the memorial marker. It's on the east side of the building in front of the parking lot.

The Armadillo Christmas Bazaar, started at the Dillo in 1976, is a popular crafts show still held each year at the Palmer Events Center.

Top: The hall was cavernous, and music fans loved it.

Bottom right: A high-rise building, housing city offices, stands on the site of the famous music hall.

Bottom left: The city put up a memorial plaque to commemorate the site in 2006.

million. Asleep at the Wheel and Commander Cody and the Lost Planet Airmen headlined the last show on New Year's Eve, 1980. Some say the music played until dawn. The Dillo was razed, and a 13-story office building rose in its place.

PRICELESS PAPERS

Where can you see the world's first photograph?

The treasures inside a modern building at 300 W. 21st St. are mind boggling to think about: 36 million pages of literary manuscripts, one million rare books, and five million photographs. Gems for the study of the arts and humanities range from a suppressed first edition of *Alice's Adventures in Wonderland* to *First Folio*, a collection of William Shakespeare's works that was published in 1623. The *Gutenberg Bible* is here. So are Bob Woodward and Carl Bernstein's notes from their Watergate investigation that helped lead to President Richard Nixon's resignation in 1974.

Harry Ransom founded the Humanities Research Center (HRC) in 1957. He began raising the resources and treasure hunting for the materials to build one of the world's greatest repositories for literary and cultural research for the United States, Europe, and Latin America. The HRC moved into its current building in 1972 to house a collection reportedly insured for more than $1 billion. With help from wealthy donors, the HRC earned a reputation for outbidding other academic rivals, including Harvard, Yale, and some very miffed, tradition-steeped, British libraries. For example, the HRC is said to have shelled out $5 million for Woodward and Bernstein's papers, including a sealed envelope that held Deep Throat's then-undisclosed identity, Mark Felt.

In the theater and performing arts, the HRC holds the papers of T. S. Eliot, Tennessee Williams, George Bernard Shaw, Arthur Miller, Peter O'Toole, Lillian Hellman, Harry Houdini, Sam Shepard, and scores of other luminaries. It has Edgar Allan Poe's

Don't miss the *Gutenberg Bible*, one of only five in the United States, and the "Niepce Heliograph," which are always on view, along with rotating exhibits.

Top right: Etched windows on the exterior of the building depict 143 highlights of the collections from Dorothea Lange's iconic Depression-era photograph, "Migrant Mother," to Dylan Thomas' poem, "Do not go gentle into that good night."

Top left: The exterior of the Harry Ransom Center

Bottom left: The world's first photograph is on permanent display.

writing desk and the sunglasses Gloria Swanson wore in the 1950 film, *Sunset Boulevard*. It has costumes and script drafts from *Gone with the Wind* and props and research material for the television series *Mad Men*. Robert De Niro's papers are here. So are John Steinbeck's archives and the journal Jack Kerouac kept in preparation for writing *On the Road*.

Ongoing exhibits showcase some of the prizes from the collections. Among the five million photographs, the world's first is kept on permanent view. Taken in France in 1827, the "Niepce Heliograph" is the earliest surviving photograph produced in the camera obscura. French innovator Joseph Niepce labored for more than a decade to produce the grainy reflective image of a garden courtyard that sits in an honored place on the ground floor of the HRC.

THE OTHER GOVERNOR'S MANSION

What Austin home almost replaced the Governor's Mansion?

Woodlawn had already been home to two former Texas governors when Lt. Gov. Bob Bullock started an effort to make it the permanent home of the state's top officeholder. The suggestion failed—reportedly neither George W. Bush nor Rick Perry wanted to leave the existing Governor's Mansion. Instead, the state sold Woodlawn to a private buyer in 2002, and it is now beautifully restored. It's a centerpiece of the Old West Austin Historic District and the Enfield neighborhood, built on the more than 365-acre grounds that once surrounded the mansion.

It's the largest of four surviving Greek Revival houses constructed by master builder Abner H. Cook, also the builder of the Governor's Mansion. After a family tragedy, the original owner, then-Texas State Comptroller James Shaw, occupied it briefly before selling it to Governor Elisha M. Pease in 1857. Pease named it Woodlawn. It was a social center of Austin in its day. Visitors included Sam Houston and George Armstrong Custer, who is said to have encamped his soldiers on the grounds.

Four generations of the Pease family lived there until it was sold to outgoing Texas Governor Allan Shivers and his wife Marialice Shary Shivers in 1957. Shivers willed it to the

Now beautifully restored, the mansion was home to two Texas governors.

University of Texas to fund a chair at the School of Law. The university sold it to the state in December, 1977, for $2.6 million. A plan to restore it to replace the Governor's Mansion faded after Bullock died in 1999. Actress Sandra Bullock was among those said to be interested in purchasing it before it was sold to entrepreneur Jeff Sandefer and his wife Laura for $2,851,100. A careful restoration by hatch + ulland owen architects removed outbuildings and additions added by the Shivers in the 1950s, but added some family-friendly features to the grounds, including a treehouse and a swimming pool.

Governor Elisha M. Pease and his wife, Lucadia Christiane Niles Pease, were from Connecticut, where the names of the Enfield neighborhood and many of the streets came from.

DID WEIRDNESS START HERE?

Why did they call it Waterloo?

That's a mystery, but a loss for Napoleon turned out to be a victory for Austin.

It's thought that Edward Burleson, the frontier military hero who surveyed the future capital city in 1838, named it Waterloo. Historians aren't exactly sure why. Napoleon met his final defeat at the town of Waterloo, Belgium, in 1815. The fearless Burleson never lost a battle. He helped lead the first assault at San Jacinto and defeated the Comanches in several fights around Austin. Maybe he liked the serene setting on the north bank of the Colorado River where the cabins of four families clustered. The name is a combination of water and the Flemish word "loo," which means "sacred wood." That perfectly fits the lake and live oak–dotted landscape of downtown Austin. It's also why Waterloo Greenway was picked as the name of the city's massive new urban greenspace. Mayor Steve Adler declared it will be "the Central Park" of Austin.

The $230 million project features a 1.5-mile greenbelt along Waller Creek from 15th Street to Lady Bird Lake. The first phase, 11-acre Waterloo Park, was scheduled to open in 2020. It includes the new Moody Amphitheater. In all, the nonprofit Waterloo Greenway Conservatory plans to redevelop 35 acres of public land for park space.

WATERLOO, HOW ARE YOU?

WHAT Waterloo Park (Scheduled to open in 2020)

WHERE Red River and East 15th Streets

COST Free

PRO TIP The trail along Waller Creek between 9th and 12th Streets lights up for the annual Creek Show, a dazzling display of light-based art installations, held in November, that draws about 50,000 visitors.

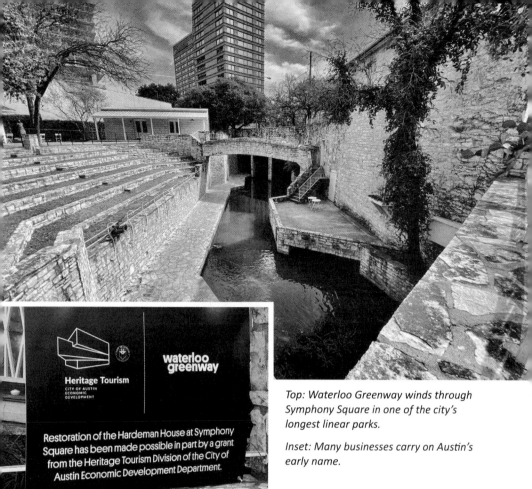

Top: Waterloo Greenway winds through Symphony Square in one of the city's longest linear parks.

Inset: Many businesses carry on Austin's early name.

In addition to the park, the city's original name is still associated with several businesses. Waterloo Ice House and Waterloo Records are some of the best known. But now it's a name that recalls the majestic beauty of the woods and waters that attracted the first settlers. Who cares if it's a little weird?

"What Central Park is to New York, Waterloo Park will be to Austin" —Mayor Steve Adler, groundbreaking ceremony, 2017.

THE DAY TIME STOOD STILL

What were the thoughts of the first reporter to see the slain sniper atop the University of Texas Tower on that historic day in August 1966?

"Charles Joseph Whitman lay in the shadow of his last afternoon."

Jerry Flemmons, our friend and fellow journalist at the *Fort Worth Star-Telegram*, wrote that lead. He saw it all firsthand himself. He was the first reporter to reach the top of the University of Texas Tower as soon as Whitman was shot fatally by Austin policeman Ramiro Martinez. Flemmons dodged rifle shots and gained access to the building. At the elevator, he saw a shaken ambulance attendant fumbling to carry a stretcher by himself. Flemmons reached out, put his hand on the stretcher, and rode up the elevator with some of the first police to access the scene. He looked on as a doctor felt for Whitman's pulse and pronounced him dead. He watched as a policeman took the sniper's driver's license from his wallet. He wrote down the name and address of the sandy-haired, crew-cut, 25-year-old UT student, a former Marine and Eagle scout.

"Get down! Get down! They're still shooting," a police lieutenant shouted at the others on the 28th floor observation deck where Whitman's body lay. On the ground, some students had fetched high-powered deer rifles from their rooms. They were still firing at what they thought was the tower gunman. "Tell them it's all over," a policeman radioed to those below. Flemmons looked at the afternoon shadow that had started to fall across

Whitman wounded more than 30 people and killed 17 on his day of rampage. The 17th victim died 35 years later from injuries sustained in the attack.

Above: The University of Texas Tower is the university's most iconic landmark.

Inset: Tours give visitors a sweeping view of Austin from the 30th floor observation deck. Photo by Marsha Miller, University of Texas at Austin

UT'S TOWERING SYMBOL

WHAT University of Texas Tower tours

WHERE Reserve and pick up tour tickets at the Texas Union Hospitality Center, 2247 Guadalupe St.; (512) 475-6636.

COST $6 per person regardless of age

PRO TIP The 45-minute self-guided tour is escorted by student guides. It is nonhistorical, focusing on the tower's architecture. Visitors ride an elevator to the 27th floor, then take three flights of stairs to the observation deck.

Whitman's body. It was seared into the lead he wrote for his front-page story in the *Star-Telegram*. He tried about 20 others before he settled on that sparse epitaph that began his report. It would be studied in journalism classes for years to come.

Flemmons saw more than his share of carnage, but as he wrote later, the Whitman shooting made him not want to be history's eyewitness any more. "That day killed my taste for violent stories," he said.

The memories of that tragic day are blissfully fading. Visitors again can ride the elevator to the heights. They look out on the sprawling campus, the capitol dome, the hills, and the graceful, shady live oaks. There are some younger folks who've never even heard the name Charles Joseph Whitman. They say time heals all wounds, but the shadow is still there.

165

BIRDS OF A FEATHER

Where can you take a stroll in a hidden oasis where peacocks flock?

Mayfield Park, tucked away at the edge of Lake Austin, is a place where flowers fly. At least it looks that way when peacocks inhabiting the park by the dozens unfurl their feathers in a kaleidoscopic fan of vibrant colors and launch onto tree branches and other perches.

This spacious, 23-acre preserve offers a creek, beautiful lily-covered koi ponds, vibrant blooming exotic flowers, and some of the most colorful birds in the world. Peacocks and peahens have been residents of the park since this estate was donated to the city in 1971. In fact, 18 varieties of peafowls live here, including India Blue and Black-shouldered. Lovely rock-framed ponds in the center of the park are surrounded with lush foliage where turtles, frogs, herons, and egrets thrive.

Like many parks in the city, this one was a gift. It was donated by the Mayfield-Gutsch Estate. Allison Mayfield was a prominent politician who served as Texas Secretary of State. He built a summer cottage on a bluff overlooking the Colorado River. When he died, his daughter, Mary Mayfield Gutsch, inherited the property and 22 adjoining undeveloped acres. She had a good vision for what the land could become and worked

GRACIOUS GROTTO

WHAT Mayfield Park

WHERE 3505 W. 35th St. Daily hours are 5 a.m. to 10 p.m.

COST Free

PRO TIP You don't have to walk far to see the peacocks. Many gather near the entrance in the morning.

Visitors to this West Austin park enjoy a lush landscape populated by peacocks.

Peacocks rule the roost at Mayfield Park, home for dozens of the colorful birds that roam the park.

with Esteban Arredondo, a gardener who spent 40 years creating and sustaining the terraced gardens and the koi-filled ponds.

You will find evidence of their partnership in the many exotic blooms in the gardens. Shades of blue, green, and pink pop in this lovely landscape. Gutsch and Arredondo also understood the importance of bringing in indigenous trees and plants to the park, ensuring a successful environment and an authentically Texan appeal. Beautiful exterior native rock walls were added. You'll find mountain laurel, redbud trees, and yucca on your stroll.

GONE TOO SOON

Why is the road named in his honor a dead end for a famous outlaw?

Sam Bass, an Indiana native and an orphan, found his way West when he was in his early twenties. He passionately wanted to be a cowboy, but financial circumstances caused him to take a job as a farmhand. He had a reputation as a hard worker; however, he had a weakness: the fast life. A lover of horses, he became a fan of horse racing and, by extension, all forms of gambling. In the West, your word is your bond, but young Sam couldn't be true. He separated a few employers from their money, leading him to search for bigger paydays. Forming a small gang, he began robbing stagecoaches in the Dallas area. The next stop was taking on trains, bringing him a huge windfall of $60,000 in newly minted gold coins.

With the bigger hauls came increased violence. This began "The Bass Wars." People were afraid of this increasing lawlessness and clamored for arrests. Even though the Texas Rangers were unable to identify Bass or most of his gang members, a lucky break with an informant led to a showdown with Bass and his boys as they prepared to rob a Round

OUTLAW AT THE CROSSROADS

WHAT Sam Bass's grave

WHERE Round Rock Cemetery, 1410 Sam Bass Rd.

COST Free

PRO TIP The outlaw's grave rests on the west side of the cemetery and is marked with a state historical marker.

Sam Bass had a brief but violent career before he was killed after attempting to rob a bank in Round Rock.

Sam Bass died on his 27th birthday after a shootout and is buried in a cemetery beside the road named for him.

Rock bank. Sam was mortally wounded, but no one claimed the honor of doing the deed for fear of revenge by gang members. Propped up by a tree one day after the shootout, Sam yelled out at passersby, "I am Sam Bass, the man that has been wanted so long." He died the next day, refusing to the end to give information about gang members. "The world is bobbing around me," were his alleged last words as he died on his 27th birthday, July 21, 1878.

In his short career, this desperado inspired widespread legends about his deeds, as well as a song, "The Ballad of Sam Bass." A wax figure in Madame Tussauds Waxworks Museum in London was unveiled. In 1988, the legend grew with the publication of *The Tenderfoot Bandits* by Paula Reed and Grover Tate. Ironically, the cemetery in which he found his final rest sits on Sam Bass Road, named after he died.

His gravestone in the Round Rock Cemetery reads, "A brave man reposes in death here. Why was he not True?"

MYSTERY OF A LOST FRENCH SHIP

How did La Salle's last ship end its journey?

Cruise ships don't dock in land-locked Austin, but that didn't stop the last ship of France's most famous explorer from landing here.

With four ships and 400 people, explorer René-Robert Cavelier Sieur de La Salle set sail for the mouth of the Mississippi in 1684 to establish a French foothold on North America. The star-crossed expedition never made it. Karankawa Indians wiped out the tiny settlement he established on the Texas coast, 400 miles from his intended destination. La Salle tried to reach the Mississippi by land, but was killed by his own men. His last ship, *La Belle*, sank at the edge of Matagorda Peninsula. Three centuries later, it was miraculously discovered. In 2014, conservators began the painstaking work of reconstructing it as a priceless exhibit at the Bullock Texas State History Museum.

It's been called one of the most important shipwrecks ever recovered. *La Belle* was in a shallow grave, in barely 14 feet of water. Marine archaeologists constructed a cofferdam to pump out the seawater around the ship and recovered it almost intact. A covering of mud preserved cargo that included everything needed to build a colony. There were muskets, swords, axes, pottery, and trade goods, including the largest cache of beads ever found in North America. Another prize was a bronze cannon decorated with dolphin-shaped handles and the crest of French King Louis IV. It was one of the first

---

The body of one of *La Belle*'s sailors, discovered when the ship was excavated, is buried at the Texas State Cemetery.

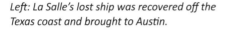

Left: La Salle's lost ship was recovered off the Texas coast and brought to Austin.

Top right: A cannon decorated with dolphins led divers to the wreck.

Bottom right: The ship was a treasure trove of goods needed to start a colony in the New World.

relics divers recovered, verifying the identity of the ship.

The French government laid claim to *La Belle* after she was found, but a compromise in 2003 resulted in a treaty that gave ownership to France and put the Texas Historical Commission in charge of her care. The ship's timbers and its relics were conserved and stabilized at the

LA BELLE'S LONG JOURNEY

WHAT *La Belle* at the Bullock Texas State History Museum

WHERE 1800 N. Congress Ave.

COST Adults, $13, seniors, $11, youth, $9

PRO TIP *Shipwrecked*, a 26-minute film with lively special effects in the museum's Spirit Theater, tells the story of a French boy, Pierre Talon, who went on the expedition with his parents, hoping to find a new home in America.

Texas A&M University Conservation Laboratory in College Station before making the trek to Austin where a large portion of the hull was reconstructed and put on view with major items from her cargo. It is the museum's most viewed exhibit.

GONE WITHOUT A PRAYER

How did the woman *Life* magazine called "the most hated woman in America" suddenly disappear?

For a woman who spent her life making headlines, Madalyn Murray O'Hair was living quietly in Austin in 1995. She was 76 and in frail health. She expected to spend an uneventful Sunday summer afternoon at her modern, one-story, glass-fronted office on the city's east side. Instead, August 27 would turn out to be the beginning of the most tragic event in her life.

Three armed men kidnapped the founder of the American Atheists group and her adult son and granddaughter. They were held for a month at a San Antonio motel before a $600,000 ransom was paid, which the kidnappers quickly converted to gold coins. The case remained open for almost six years. In 2001, David Roland Waters, a convicted felon who once managed O'Hair's office, led investigators to the remains of the O'Hairs, buried on a remote, 5,000-acre West Texas ranch.

Waters died in a North Carolina prison from lung cancer just two years after his confession, which included a detailed account of the crime, released after his death. The O'Hair kidnapping was the subject of a Netflix movie, *The Most*

THE MYSTERIOUS END OF MADALYN MURRAY

WHAT Former world headquarters of the American Atheists

WHERE 7215 Cameron Rd.

PRO TIP O'Hair's remains were cremated and buried at an undisclosed site in Central Texas by her son, Bill Murray. She once said she wanted just three words on her epitaph: "Woman, Atheist, Anarchist."

Madalyn Murray was last seen at her Austin office on a Sunday in 1995.

Hated Woman in America, which premiered at the city's South by Southwest (SXSW) festival in 2017.

O'Hair landed in Austin in 1965 after living in Houston and Baltimore, where she filed the landmark suit that helped abolish organized prayer and Bible reading in public schools. She worked unsuccessfully to have "In God We Trust" removed from coins and "Under God" removed from the Pledge of Allegiance. She ran unsuccessfully for city council in the late 1970s. She opened the American Atheist headquarters in 1988 at an estimated cost of $1.7 million. Waters, who had access to her books, believed she had more than $3 million hidden in foreign accounts.

The building has had several tenants since American Atheists relocated its headquarters to New Jersey in 1998.

TWO CADDIES WHO CHANGED THE GAME

How did a couple of caddies help save the city's most beloved golf course?

They were just two young caddies who sneaked onto the course and started playing golf one day in 1950. But what they did changed the game forever.

"Let them play," Austin Mayor Taylor Glass said simply. The golf course manager had called the city to ask what to do when the two African American youths were discovered on the course. No other golf course in the South was integrated. By that simple act, Lions Municipal Golf Course, nicknamed Muny, became the first. It was one of the reasons the beloved course was included on the National Register of Historic Places in 2016. That same year, the National Trust for Historic Preservation put it on its list of 11 most endangered historic sites in America. The University of Texas, which owns the bucolic 171-acre tract dotted with ancient live oaks, has been making plans to develop it.

Save Muny stepped in. It reminded people of some of the legendary golfers who've played there—Ben Hogan, Tom Kite, Harvey Penick, Sandra Haynie, Byron Nelson, and many others. Ben Crenshaw, who's helped in the design of some of the world's greatest golf courses, offered a plan to redesign Muny for free. The two-time Master's winner had a special

SAVING MUNY

WHAT Lions Municipal Golf Course

WHERE 2901 Enfield Rd.

COST Weekday greens fees are $31.

PRO TIP The Firecracker Open, held the first week in July, is one of the state's oldest amateur tournaments. Tom Kite, who grew up playing Muny, won it in 1968. The 75th tournament will be held in 2021, if Muny survives.

A lion on the putting green is a namesake of the course, operated by the Lions Club before the city took over. The golf course is listed on the National Register of Historic Places, which also warned that it is one of the most endangered historic sites in America.

attachment for the course. He grew up three blocks away, and it's where he learned to play. More than that, it's where he learned to love the game.

"My story is no different than that of countless other youngsters eager to play the game, but we were provided a lovely place in which these memories will last us a lifetime," Crenshaw said. "I regard these memories as irreplaceable."

The Lions Municipal Golf Course is part of the 503-acre tract George Brackenridge gave the University of Texas in 1910 in hopes of relocating the entire campus to the picturesque site on the shore of what is now Lady Bird Johnson Lake.

FREE-RANGE CHICKENS

How can you possibly update an age-old Bingo game?

Rockabilly country music and ice-cold beer are calling cards for the Little Longhorn Saloon, a small bar filled with neon signs and memorabilia. Self-named "the honkiest tonkiest beer joint in Texas," the bar swings for the fences in that area. Well-known country-and-western bands such as the Derailers and Two Hoots and a Holler, as well as favorite performers such as Weldon Henson and James Hand, pack the place. Another part of the bar's popularity is the "six days a week" happy hour. On a hot summer day, patrons enjoy draft beer for $1.50. The owners Terry and David Gaona have been true to the "dive bar" ethos. Lots of cold brew, but don't ask for a Cosmopolitan.

Separating itself from regular country music bars, the big draw is Chicken Sh*t Bingo. The idea came to Austin from California. The West Coast version of the game involved cows, but the original owners of the Austin bar went for a smaller approach—chickens. Make a donation and get a ticket bearing your hopefully lucky numbers. Wait in line and then it's feeding time for the avian shot callers. A lot of chicken feed hits the Bingo board, which soon translates into Bingo card marking. Loretta Lynn, the chicken, has been one of the well-known excretory contributors at the games. She never disappoints. If your number is the lucky recipient of the fowl's largesse, you win a prize. Lucky folks go home waving

---

The unique Bingo game can get you a picture in the Chicken Sh*t Hall of Fame, if you're lucky. If you're not the winner, it's still a rollicking great time.

The Little Longhorn Saloon is famous for chickens that call the shots in its long running Bingo game.

WATCH YOUR STEP

WHAT Chicken Sh*t Bingo at the Little Longhorn Saloon

WHERE 5434 Burnet Rd. on Sundays from 4 to 8 p.m.

COST Donation of $2 gets you a ticket. Children are welcome for Sunday night Bingo.

PRO TIP Bingo starts at 4 p.m. Get there early for a good seat and a chance at a good Bingo ticket. Stay later for a great deal on $2 beer.

a handful of long green, $114 to be exact. Winners get a picture on the wall for posterity, as well as being inducted into the Chicken Sh*t Hall of Fame. If you don't get your number marked on the first chicken run, don't despair. The Bingo game has four to eight sessions each Sunday night. This is the only time that the saloon will allow children on the premises.

ICONIC FIGURES IN STONE

Who was the rebellious woman who brought history's heroes to life?

Stepping into Elisabet Ney's castle-like home and studio is like entering a salon filled with famous people. Everywhere you look, there are statues and busts of legendary figures—Sam Houston, Stephen F. Austin, and many others.

Almost hidden away on a quiet neighborhood street in Hyde Park, the Elisabet Ney Museum showcases the life's work of the celebrated sculptress. Ney was a sought-after classical artist in Germany when she and her husband immigrated to the United States during the Franco-Prussian War. Ney was considered rebellious on both sides of the Atlantic. She was a rare female sculptress in Germany. In America, she wore bloomers to garden and went by her own name, instead of her husband's.

Ney's fortunes ascended after she was selected to sculpt the likenesses of Sam Houston and Stephen F. Austin for the Chicago World Fair in 1893. The Texas legislature awarded her $32,000 to fund the work.

She built a two-story limestone house in 1892 that she named "Formosa," Portuguese for "beautiful." In her day, it was a fortress at the edge of the city. The grounds are planted in wildflowers and native plants to look like they did in the days when Formosa was a gathering place for artists and art appreciators.

WHERE HEROES STAND TALL

WHAT Elisabet Ney Museum

WHERE 304 E. 44th. Open Wednesday to Sunday, noon to 5 p.m.

COST Admission is free. Donations welcomed.

PRO TIP Ney, an early feminist who was very dedicated to her work, died in her studio on June 29, 1907.

Top: Elisabet Ney built *Formosa* at the edge of Austin. Now it's a museum listed on the National Register of Historic Places in Hyde Park.

Inset: Plaster casts and busts of Elisabet Ney's sculptures fill the studio.

Plaster casts on view at the museum give visitors a close-up view of one of the challenges Ney faced in memorializing the two Texas heroes: Austin was 5-foot-7. Houston was 6-foot-2. To give the Father of Texas equal footing, Ney posed his statue on a higher pedestal. The finished marble statues stand in honored places in the state capitol and in Statuary Hall at the nation's capitol. Determined to perfect her work, Ney missed the deadline for the Chicago celebration, so World's Fair visitors didn't get to see them.

On guided tours, well-informed docents provide visitors with many other insights about the remarkable life of the artist who gave her adopted city a vision of history carved in stone.

You can enjoy the artist's work while exploring the beautiful castle-like studio where she lived.

TOP SECRET VODKA

What vodka maker's distillery is as secret as a moonshine still?

There are no tours and no signs on the buildings. It takes a diligent search to find the sprawling complex in far southeast Austin that houses Tito's Handmade Vodka. Ten floor-to-ceiling stills on the 24-acre site produce more than 850,000 cases annually. It's enough to give founder Bert "Tito" Beveridge, a former geologist, a net worth of more than $2.5 billion in 2017, according to *Forbes* magazine.

That's a lot of handmade hooch. But a pair of lawsuits claiming it was too much to make by hand were tossed out in 2016. Tito maintains the process hasn't changed since he opened the first legal distillery in Texas in 1997. It was a long uphill battle. Tito began by researching moonshine

---

THE FIRST TEXAS DISTILLERY

WHAT Tito's Handmade Vodka

WHERE 12101 Moore Rd. and the downtown Love, Tito's store, at 215 Lavacca St.

COST Tito's gifts start at $10.

PRO TIP Tito's Vodka has profited not only from word of mouth from loyal fans but also from a wealth of product placement. Watch any reality show on television and see if you can find a bottle of Tito's.

Tito's distillery doesn't give tours, but videos and other information tell the company's story at www.titosvodka.com/titos-story. A new downtown retail store at 215 Lavaca St. opened in 2020. The Love, Tito's store, sells many gift items, with proceeds going to charity, but it doesn't sell liquor.

Top left and bottom right: The Love, Tito's retail store, sells gift items, but not liquor.

Bottom left and top right: The company's production facility sprawls across 24 acres in southeast Austin but isn't open for tours.

stills that proliferated during Prohibition. He plastered old photos of Texas Rangers raiding stills around a one-room workshop he called "The Shack." He used a pair of Dr Pepper kegs and an outdoor turkey fryer to fire up his first still. Rather than the potato base most vodkas were made with, Tito used yellow corn.

When investors turned him down, he financed operations with a fistful of credit cards that he maxed out for $88,000. He was a one-man company. "I'd go out and make it and sell it and come back and make some more," he recalls. The tide turned in 2001 when Tito shipped off a couple of bottles to the World Spirits Competition in San Francisco. He was too busy to go himself, but his vodka spoke for itself. It won a double gold medal over 72 other entries.

QUEEN BEE

Who is the mystery woman standing on top of the state capitol, and did she really have a beehive in her nose?

First of all, who would want to have a nose big enough to hold a beehive? Pundits have never been kind to the 16-foot *Goddess of Liberty* statue that tops the capitol dome. It's true that she has a nose as big as a football. Her lips and eyes are outsized too. She was made that way so she would look good 311 feet in the air. Not long after she was installed in 1888, a local reporter called her "Old Lady Goddess." No one was even sure she was a goddess. About the nicest thing said about her was that she looked better from a distance.

That's not to say she isn't loved. Many Texans are crazy about her. Even schoolchildren chipped in to give her a total makeover and craft a new stand-in that was airlifted atop the capitol by helicopter in 1986. An inspection in 1983 found the original too frail for further service after standing out in the sun and rain for 97 years. Her background was questionable. Detroit architect Elijah E. Meyers included a statue in his original design for the capitol, but no one is sure what kind of symbol he had in mind. Some said he might have been influenced by the *Statue of Liberty* under construction in New York Harbor at the time. The Chicago firm of Friedley and Voshardt brought plaster molds to Austin in January 1888 and set up a foundry to cast an Amazonian-size

READY FOR HER CLOSE UP

WHAT *Goddess of Liberty*

WHERE Restored original at the Bob Bullock Texas State History Museum, 1800 Congress Ave., and replica atop the nearby Texas State Capitol

COST Admission to the Bullock Museum: $13 adults, $11 seniors 65+, $9 youth 4-17

PRO TIP Parking is $10 at the Bullock Museum Parking Garage, and the capitol is within walking distance, if you want to visit both.

The original goddess is a little startling when you see her up close at the Bullock Museum.

woman made of zinc alloy. She held a sword in one hand and her upraised right hand held a star gilded in gold.

The goddess was brought back to earth by a Texas National Guard helicopter. After a thorough examination, the Sculpture Conservation Laboratory at Washington Technology Associates, Inc. in St. Louis recommended replacement. Delray Bronze in Houston made an exact replica. The new goddess toured six Texas cities before she was gently put back on her high perch by a Mississippi National Guard "Skyhook" helicopter as thousands watched.

The original 3,000-pound goddess was painstakingly restored by American Art Foundry in Rhome, Texas. After she was finished, she toured Fort Worth and the State Fair of Texas before returning to Austin. Today she stands in an honored place at Bob Bullock Texas State History Museum. Her nose is as big as it always was, but she's indoors now and at least there aren't any bees to worry about.

The *Goddess of Liberty* still stands tall, despite the stings of critics and bees.

HOUSE OF JOY

Where's the best place in the city to spend a quiet moment?

In a downtown area that buzzes with music on almost every corner, artist Ellsworth Kelly created an art installation as big as a church for quiet contemplation. It's the most monumental artwork he ever did and it was one of the final major projects of his life. He called it *Austin.*

Opened in 2018, *Austin* is the cornerstone of the Blanton Museum of Art, one of the largest university art museums in the nation. Kelly gifted the design, and generous contributions from the University of Texas and art patrons Jeanne and Mickey Klein funded the building of the 2,715-square-foot chapel. The soft white exterior constructed with Spanish limestone glimmers under a blue Texas sky. Inside, the walls are awash with vibrant colors from stained glass windows that change patterns like a kaleidoscope with the day's changing light. "It's like being inside a Kelly painting come to life," *Vanity Fair* magazine reported when it opened.

Museum director Simone Wicha, who led the effort to bring the chapel to Austin, said, "a work of this scale by an artist of this magnitude is once in a lifetime." Kelly envisioned it as a place for joy and contemplation. Mission accomplished.

The white limestone chapel glimmers like a moonscape under the blue Texas sky.

Artist Ellsworth Kelly gave his biggest gift to a city he loved from a distance, but never visited.

BABY FACE AND THE BLUE BONNET COURT

Did Public Enemy No. 1 hide out in the city's oldest motor court?

His real name was Lester Joseph Gillis. In his youth, friends nicknamed him "Baby Face Nelson." However, it was best not to call him that unless you wanted to wind up on the wrong end of a Thompson submachine gun. He liked "Jimmy" better. Or "Les." Was he part of the suspicious-looking gang of four men and a woman in two cars who rolled into the Blue Bonnet Tourist Camp on a quiet day in the midst of the Great Depression?

Gaye Lucas thinks so. His grandparents, Joe and Elizabeth "Miss Bessie" Lucas, built the 11-room motel in 1928. Besides running the tourist court, Joe was a deputy sheriff. Miss Bessie didn't like the looks of the strangers. Joe cradled a shotgun in the crook of his arm and politely asked them to leave. They vanished in the middle of the night. Fortunately, Joe had scratched down their license plate numbers. Gaye says it matched cars the authorities were looking for.

Baby Face went on to many robberies and shootouts until he was gunned down by FBI agents at Barrington, Illinois, on November 27, 1934. He was 25. The FBI had recently elevated him to Public Enemy No. 1.

The Blue Bonnet Tourist Camp, which became the Blue Bonnet Court, lasted a whole lot longer. Austin's oldest motor court was listed on the National Register of Historic Places in 1990. It was the setting for a prize-winning play, *Blue Bonnet Court*, written by Zsa Zsa Gershick, which premiered at the Hudson Theatre in Los Angeles in 2006. The Blue Bonnet sign

Blue Bonnet Court was one of the first motor courts built in Austin.

out front is said to be the city's first neon sign. These days it no longer shines and is missing most of its tubing. The Blue Bonnet is showing its age, but fortunately no bullet holes. It operates as budget-priced efficiency lodging.

Baby Face Nelson stood 5-foot-4. He died in a blast of gunfire with the FBI.

A SIMPLE HOWDY

Did you know that all you need is a little love to survive?

Jeremiah the Innocent has lingered on the side of a wall at 21st Street and Guadalupe since the mural was commissioned in 1993 by the now-defunct record store, the Sound Garden. The business paid the muralist $90 and set him loose on the building's exterior with the instructions, do whatever you want to. His choice: a kindly frog with prominent eyes sharing an Austin-style greeting.

The artist for the mural was the musician who had created the image 10 years earlier. Made popular by a Kurt Cobain T-shirt, this piece of street art is known as "Hi, how are you?" The subject of the mural, a quizzical frog, was on the cover of an alternative rock album by musician Daniel Johnston. Johnston chose the simple illustration for the cover of his record. The figure gained unexpected popularity, ending up on the store's exterior wall. The artist referred to his art as *Jeremiah, the Innocent Frog*.

People find their way to the site, located across the street from the University of Texas. Its friendly message encourages visitors to stop for a photo or two as a memento of a trip to a laid-back Austin. The mural almost didn't survive when the downturn in the popularity of vinyl (before its current resurgence) led to new tenants in the building who planned to obliterate it. Fans in the area stepped up and put an end to the plans.

An Austin fixture, Johnston was well known for passing out cassette tapes of his music at the hamburger restaurant where

FRIENDLY FROG

WHAT Hi, how are you? mural

WHERE 21st and Guadalupe Streets

COST Free

PRO TIP Daniel Johnson, who did not enjoy financial success as an artist in life, is now being celebrated by the high-end clothing brand Supreme, a division of the group that also owns Louis Vuitton. His artwork will emblazon hoodies, work pants, and t-shirts.

Rain or shine, Jeremiah greets you on the Drag.

he worked. Jeremiah made his debut on the cover of Johnson's *Unfinished Album* in 1983. The artist who has had songs covered by Tom Waits and Beck was diagnosed with mental illness and was hospitalized in treatment for his condition, but that didn't deter him from his musical career. His influence was strong enough in the music community to inspire two documentaries made about his life while his artwork has been shown at the Whitney Museum. The affection for the little frog and the spirit behind it brought about a declaration by Austin Mayor Steve Adler, marking January 22 "Mental Wellness Day."

The artist Daniel Johnston died in September 2019.

SOURCES

Alright, Alright, Alright
https://parade.com/267634/ashleighschmitz/alright-alright-alright-watch-the-most-buzzed-about-oscar-acceptance-speeches/

Too Big to Deliver
"Greetings from Austin Mural in Austin, Texas," 2019. Silly America. www.sillyamerica.com
"Vintage Style Neon Art, Handmade in Texas." www.roadhouserelics.com

The Big Byte
"Michael Dell, Taking the Direct Approach." www.entrepreneur.com

Arachnophobes, Beware
Jeff Bell. "Austin's Mueller Neighborhood to Open 8th New Park." September 11, 2019. www.kvue.com
"Arachnophilia," Museum Without Walls. www.culturenow.com

Bevo Settles an Old Score
"The Truth about Bevo," www.texasexes.org/about-us/history-and-traditions.

A Garden Older Than Dirt
Austin Home & Living, July/August 2002.

Discovering a Pearl
www.threadgills.com

A Texas-Size Bat
Museum without Walls. www.culturenow.org
Shelley Bueche. "History of Austin's Famous Congress Avenue's Bats Flies from Hysteria to City Treasure." May 4, 2018. https://austin.culturemap.com

Custer Rode to the Rescue
Coppedge, Clay, "Custer in Texas," February 23, 2011.
Dippie, Brian W., *The Handbook of Texas Online*, www.tshaonline.org/handbook/online/articles/fcu36
George Armstrong Custer, www.texasescapes.com

Books with a View
"Sneak Peak: An Early Tour of Austin's New Central Library," *Austin American-Statesman*, October 24, 2017.

Talk This Way, Please
Austin American-Statesman, Sept. 27, 2019.
McLeod, Marilyn, "Manchaca Was Not Named after Jose Menchaca," Manchaca Onion Creek Historical Society, Feb. 28, 2018.

Austin's Long Road Home
"A Guide to the Austin Papers." Briscoe Center for American History.
https://legacy.lib.utexas.edu/taro/utcah/00359/cah-00359.html

It Keeps on Ticking
Gracy, David B. Handbook of Texas Online; www.tshaonline.org/handbook/articles, August, 2010.
AustinTexas/George-Washington-Littlefield-Building. www.texasescapes.com

Cleared to Land
"Austin Historic Landmark Commission," by Jay Janner, *Austin American-Statesman*, Feb. 27, 2018.

End of the Road for Geraldine
Bueche, Shelly "The Funky History of Rainey Street," https://austinculturemap.com, June 14, 2019.

Sainted Oil
Weaver, Bobby. "The Well that Launched the Permian." *PB Oil&Gas Magaine*. October 12, 2017.
https://pboilandgasmagazine.com/the-well-that-launched-the-permian/

Why They Call it "Dirty's"
Austin American-Statesman, April 30, 1991.
"The Burger Hall of Fame," *Texas Monthly* July 20, 2016.
Martin's Kum-Bak Place, *Community Impact Newspaper*, Nov. 29, 2018.

You're Guilty, but We'll Name the Courthouse after You
"Henry's Pennies," www.riversidecemeterync.wordpress.com.
"O.Henry," www.en.wikipedia.org

A Puzzling Picture

Largey, Matt. KUT "Why does the top of Austin's largest building look unfinished?" July 15, 2019. www.kut.org

Widner, Cindy. @CurbedAustin. "Tour the Independent, Austin's new tallest tower." August 30, 2019. www.austin.curbed.com

Foam Sweet Foam

Russell, Erin. "Historic Downtown Beer Garden Revamps with Former Frank Owner." March 22, 2019. www.austin.eater.com

Weible, David. "Scholz Garten in Austin, Texas." www.savingplaces.org.

Turn on the Moonlight

Prince, Jackson. "The Complete Guide to Austin's Moonlight Towers." March 26, 2018. www.austinot.com

A Carnivore's Delight

Thompson, Paul. "Owner of Sam's BBQ, a longtime East Austin eatery, wrestles with $5 million offer from an Oregon developer." October 18, 2018. *Austin Business Journal.* www.bizjournals.com

"What's Next for Sam's BBQ?" July 2019. *Austin Monthly.* www.austinmonthly.com

No Limits

"What is Austin City Limits?" History of ACL. www.acltv.com

Groceries From the Golden Days

Avenue B Grocery and Market. www.avenuebgrocery.com

Avenue B Grocery and Market. www.austin.culturemap.com

Mosaic Mystery

Faires, Robert. "Your Essential Magnificence." September 16, 2011. *Austin Chronicle.* www.austinchronicle.com

Mikulski, Tim. "Your Essential Magnificence in Austin, Texas." March 27, 2013. *Americans for the Arts.* www.blog.americansforthearts.org

Margarita with a View

"Oasis Restaurant." www.en.wikipedia.org

Casa Neverlandia

David J. Jeff and Chelle Neff. *Weird Homes: The People and Places that Keep Austin Strangely Wonderful.* Skyhorse Publishing. 2018.

Penick, Pam. "Casa Neverlandia and Sculpture by James Talbot Jeep Austin Delightfully Weird." October 10, 2019. *Digging: Cool Gardens in a Hot Climate.* www.penick.net.

Rock of Ages

"Historic Landmarks." Clarksville Community Development Corporation. www.clarksvillecdc.org

Double Trouble

Corcoran, Michael. "Gone 20 Years, Stevie Ray Vaughan Stands Forever Tall in Austin." September 23, 2018. www.austin360.com

An Alamo Survivor's Story

The Handbook of Texas Online. Austintexas.gov/page/about-susanna-dickinson-museum; https://tshaonline.org/handbook/online

Charles Umlauf's Secret Garden

www.umlaufsculpture.org

There's No Pool Like an Old Pool

Friends of Deep Eddy, www.deepeddy.org.

Music for a General on Mount Bonnell

The Handbook of Texas Online, Mount Bonnell, Seldon B. Graham, July 20, 2015; www.wikipedia.org/wiki/Mount-Bonnell

The Queen of Oratory

Faires, Robert. "Barbara Jordan Statue: Standing Like She Stood Up for the Constitution." www.austinchronicle.com/arts/2007-07-06/499190/

Hank's Last Show

Evans, Rush. "Separate Truth from Fiction in Country Icon Hank Williams' Final Days," April 21, 2010. *Goldmine, the Music Collector's Magazine.*

The Flood That Lifted up Whole Foods

"Repaying the Favor. Whole Foods Offers Loans to Flooded Shoal Creek Businesses," by Michael Theis, May 27, 2015. *Austin Business Journal.*

"Whole Foods Market," *Encyclopedia Britannica,* www.britannica.com/topic/whole-foods-market.

How the State Flower Lost Its Thorns
"Bluebonnets" *Texas Tales* column, Mike Cox, March 30, 2006.

Be Wary of Hairy
"Is the Hairy Man Bumping about in Round Rock," *Austin American-Statesman*, June 12, 2017.
"Williamson County Cuts Back on Number of Trees Needing to Be Removed on Hairy Man Road." FOX 7 Austin, Dec. 31, 2019.

A Window on the World
St. Mary's Cathedral: Diocese of Austin. www.smcaustin.org

Comedy Meets Magic
www.esthersfollies.com
Wassenich, Red. *Keeping Austin Weird*. Schaffer Publishing, 2016.

Chips Off the Old Block
"Bremond Block Historic District (Austin, Texas)," www.en.wikipedia.org
Karney, Sarah. "A Visual Tour of Austin's Historic Bremond Block," March 4, 2017. *Culture Trip.* www.culturetrip.com

Heaven for Foodies
Jernigan, Joleen. "The Thicket Is Austin's Most Underrated Food Truck Park." October 16, 2019. www.austinot.com
www.thepicnicaustin.com

A Rocky Reception
Dashi, Dahlia. Actual Factual WilCo. "How Did Round Rock Get Its Name?" September 22, 2018. www.statesman.com
"The Round Rock Story." www.roundrockchamber.org

Reddy Kilowatt Would Be Proud
Austin, Texas: Grotto Wall at Sparky Park. Roadside America. www.roadsideamerica.com
Dragna, Madison. "Sparky Park in Austin, Texas Is the Pocket Park with Unbeatable Charm." March 6, 2018. www.tripstodiscover.com

Country Music Spoken Here
www.brokenspokeaustintx.net
Hall, Michael, "Accommodating an Old Honky Tonk in New Austin," January 12, 2013. *New York Times.*

Equine Royalty
"Alexander Proctor and Seven Mustangs." www.eastfoundation.net

First Lady
"'Leanderthal Lady' Lives on Decades after Her Discovery," March 28, 2019. *Community Impact Newspaper*
www.texasbeyondhistory.net.

It's a Bird, It's a Plane, It's a Dinosaur
Wagner, Stephen. "Are Pterodactyl Sightings Real?" January 6, 2019.
https://www.liveabout.com/did-pterosaurs-survive-extinction-2594566
Texas Memorial Museum, https://tmm.utexas.edu. The University of Texas at Austin Jackson School of Geosciences, www.jsg.utexas.edu/news/files/NFD
University of Bristol. "The rise and rise of the flying reptiles: Pterosaurs not driven into extinction by birds, study reveals." ScienceDaily. ScienceDaily, July 7, 2011.
<www.sciencedaily.com/releases/2011/07/110706101608.htm>

Star Maker
"Joanna Troutman" Texas State Cemetery.
https://cemetery.tspb.texas.gov/pub/user_form.asp?pers_id=108
Hazlewood, Claudia. "Troutman, Joanna." TSHA Online.
https://tshaonline.org/handbook/online/articles/ftr13

Clara's Heavenly Lagoon
"Laguna Gloria," *Texas Highways*, February 2017.

Friendly Flora
Phillips, Hannah. "A History of Mueller Sun Flowers in 60 Seconds." June 18, 2019.

Tragedy of a Tree
Parker, Mike. "25 Years Later, Intrigue of Poisoned Treaty Oak Remains." September 26, 2018. Statesman.com.

Strollin' Down the River

Gugino, Amber. "Newest Installation of Public Art Project at 2nd and Guadalupe." April 22, 2015.
http://downtownaustinblog.org/category/austin-art/
"Reflections on the Brazos." Museum without Walls. www.culturenow.org

A Blonde Icon

Garcia, Jose. "Mosaic Artist Brings Austinites into the Larger Picture of Her Work." June 24, 2017.
www.thedailytexan.com. Installed 2017.

The Chitlin' Circuit

"The Historic Victory Grill/Historic Premier Blues Club." Austin's East End Cultural Heritage District.
http://www.eastendculturaldistrict.org

Servant Girl Annihilator

Letter to Dave included in O. Henry. *Rolling Stones*, short story compilation, 1912.
"The Servant Girl Murders. Austin, Texas, 1885," www.servantgirlmurders.com

The Spirits of the Driskill

Berry, MarLee. "Three Things You Might Not Know about Austin's Famous Driskill Hotel."
September 20, 2017. www.texashillcountry.com

Discovering the Dinos

"Dinosaur Tracks in Leander." www.athomeinleander.com
Judson, Olivia. "When Texas Was at the Bottom of the Sea." January 2015. www.smithsonianmag.com
Lawrence, Katie. "The Mystical Place in Texas Where Dinosaurs Once Roamed." May 28, 2018.
www.onlyinyourstate.com

Cerveza and Legends

Ayala, Christine. "Drink in History at Some of Austin's Bars." *Austin American-Statesman*. July 9, 2014

Don't Come and Take It

"Angelina Eberly." www.capitalareastatues.com.

Sway to the Smoky Sweet Blues

Moser, Margaret. "The Scene Is Gone but Not Forgotten." August 9, 1996. *Austin Chronicle*.
www.austinchronicle.com.

A Balancing Act

Ketterer, Samantha . "New 50-Foot-Tall Sculpture Makes Wave on Campus." January 22, 2015. *The Daily Texan*. www.thedailytexan.com

The Pig War

Coppedge, Clay, "The Pig War," by TexasEscapes.com, Jan. 1, 2011.
The Handbook of Texas Online, "Dubois De Saligny," by Nancy Barker, June 12, 2010.

Aggies Stormed the Castle

"Our Story." Tinkertown Museum. http://tinkertown.com/?page_id=2; "Tinkertown." Roadside America.
https://www.roadsideamerica.com/story/11018; site visit, September 20, 2019.

Think or Swim

"Salon of the West," *The Austin Chronicle*, July 4, 2003, Steve Moore.

Home of the Hilltoppers

"St. Edwards-University," https://en.wikipedia.org/wiki/St._Edward%27s_University

The Paramount Still Shines

"Paramount Theatre History,"
www.austintheatre.org/about-us/paramount-theatre/paramount-history/

Convict Hill Left Its Mark

Buchanan, Taylor Jackson, "The History behind the Name Convict Hill in South Austin," *Community Impact Newspaper*, Oct. 25, 2018.
McGlinchy, Audrey, KUT(/People/Audrey-McGlinchy-KUT) "Were There Convicts on Convict Hill?"
May 11, 2017.

The Day the Dillo Died

Webber, Andrew, www.awhq.com; "Remembering the Armadillo World Headquarters,"
Dec. 30, 2015. www.KUT.org.
www.wikipedia.org/wiki/Armadillo-World-Headquarters.

Priceless Papers

Max, D. T. Letter from Austin Final Destination, *The New Yorker*, June 11 and 18, 2007.

The Other Governor's Mansion

"A Little Fixer-Upper," *Austin Chronicle*, Nov. 9, 2001.
"Pease Mansion again Up for Sale," *Austin American-Statesman*, Aug. 20, 2002.

Did Weirdness Start Here?

Freer, Emma, "Downtown Austin Parks District Named Waterloo Greenway," *Community Impact Newspaper*, Aug. 22, 2019.

Hazelwood, Claudia, "Waterloo, Tx," *Handbook of Texas Online*, by, June 15, 2010.

The Day Time Stood Still

Curmudgeon in Corduroy: The Best of Jerry Flemmons' Texas, TCU Press, 2000.

"Former AP Writer Mike Cochran Recalls Serving as Oswald's Pallbearer," *Lubbock Avalanche-Journal*, Nov. 21, 2013, by Mike Cochran.

Birds of a Feather

Barnes, Michael. "Partnership Nurtured Mayfield Park Gardens." September 27, 2018. *Statesman*. www.statesman.com

Prothro, Rowan, and Carter, Casey, "Mayfield Park and Nature Preserve." Texas A&M AgriLife Extension. www.txmn.tamu.edu

Gone Too Soon

"The Story of Sam Bass. The Historic Round Rock Collection: An Ongoing History." www.roundrocktexas.gov

Mystery of a Lost French Ship

www.storyoftexas.com/la-belle/the-exhibit.

Gone without a Prayer

MacCormick, John, "Archive, O'Hair's Last Days," *San Antonio Express*, March 2, 2017.

"Madalyn Murray O'Hair Timeline," *Austin Chronicle*, Nov. 20, 1998.

Two Caddies Who Changed the Game

Courtney, David, "Save Muny," *Texas Monthly*, April 2017.

Free-Range Chickens

Phillips Hanna, "Chicken Sh*t Bingo Is Really a Thing and Here's Why," January 9, 2019. www.theculturetrip.com

Iconic Figures in Stone

Elisabet Ney Biography. Austin Parks and Recreation. www.austintexas.gov

Top Secret Vodka

"Inside Tito's Vodka: How a Man Named Beveridge Built a 2.5 Billion Fortune," Oct. 17, 2017. www.forbes.com. www.titosvodka.com/tito's-story "The Troubling Success of Tito's Handmade Vodka," *Forbes Magazine*, June 26, 2013.

Queen Bee

www.thestoryoftexas.com/discover/texas-state-capitol/goddess-liberty

House of Joy

"How Austin Became the Home, and Namesake of Ellsworth Kelly's Final Masterpiece," *Vanity Fair*, February, 2018.

Baby Face and the Blue Bonnet Court

"Blue Bonnet Court, Austin Tx," www.roadsidepeek.com/roadusa/southwest/texas/texasmotel/texasothermotel/bluebonnet/index.htm.

Janaes, Eileen. "The Battle of Barrington." *Country Magazine*. April 10, 2015. https://jwcdaily.com/countrymag/2015/04/10/the-battle-of-barrington/

A Simple Howdy

Hoffberger, Chase. "Thai, How Are You?" August 28, 2013. *The Austin Chronicle*. www.austinchronicle.com.

Prince, Jackson. "Everything You Don't Know about the Best Murals in Austin." February 18, 2018. *The Austinot*. www.austinot.com

INDEX